Easy-to-Follow
Mediterranean Diet
Cookbook for Beginners

*A Comprehensive Cookbook with a 30-Day Meal Plan
to Explore the Vibrant Flavors of the Mediterranean
and Experience the Wholesome Lifestyle*

Brandi K. Newton

CONTENTS

Vegetable Mains And Meatless Recipes

Sides , Salads, And Soups Recipes..44

Beans , Grains, And Pastas Recipes..52

Fruits, Desserts And Snacks Recipes 63

Appendix : Recipes Index 72

INTRODUCTION

Brandi K. Newton, acclaimed nutritionist and passionate food enthusiast, brings to your table the essence of the Mediterranean lifestyle - a harmonious blend of fresh ingredients, age-old traditions, and health-enhancing recipes. Drawing inspiration from sun-kissed shores, olive groves, and bustling coastal markets, this cookbook invites you to delve deep into the rich tapestry of Mediterranean cuisine, where food is more than sustenance; it's a celebration.

This cookbook encapsulates Brandi's passion for the richly diverse and heart-healthy Mediterranean diet, offering an inviting introduction to its staples and traditions.

For centuries, the Mediterranean region's inhabitants have thrived on a diet abundant in fresh fruits and vegetables, whole grains, legumes, lean proteins, and heart-healthy fats, woven together with the vibrant threads of their local herbs and spices. Recognized for its numerous health benefits, from heart health to cognitive wellbeing, this diet is more than a fleeting trend—it's a sustainable lifestyle that promotes long-term health and vitality.

In this cookbook, Brandi artfully combines the science of nutrition with the art of cooking. Each recipe is a celebration of the Mediterranean diet's flavorful bounty, crafted with love and a deep understanding of the diet's nutritional philosophy. Whether you're a seasoned cook or stepping into the world of Mediterranean cuisine for the first time, these recipes are approachable, varied, and undeniably delicious, designed to inspire and facilitate your journey towards healthier living.

Enjoy the journey through this cookbook, where each page invites you to explore the tastes, textures, and wholesome benefits of the Mediterranean diet. May it lead you towards vibrant health, delicious meals, and joyful moments shared around your table. Welcome to your Mediterranean journey. Enjoy the ride and Buon Appetito!

The Mediterranean Diet is a nutritional pattern and lifestyle inspired by the traditional dietary habits of some of the countries bordering the Mediterranean Sea, including Italy, Greece, Spain, and southern France. It's not merely a diet in the conventional sense of a temporary regimen; it's a long-term approach to eating that can be enjoyed over a lifetime.

Key Components of the Mediterranean Diet

Whole Foods: A focus on fresh, seasonal, and minimally processed foods.

Fruits and Vegetables: These are foundational and consumed in abundance, providing essential vitamins, minerals, and dietary fiber.

Healthy Fats: Particularly olive oil, which replaces butter and other unhealthy fats. Nuts and seeds are also sources of healthy fats and are consumed regularly.

Whole Grains: Instead of refined grains, whole grains like whole wheat, brown rice, barley, and quinoa are staples.

Lean Proteins: Fish and seafood are consumed at least twice a week. Poultry, eggs, cheese, and yogurt are consumed in moderation, while red meat is limited.

Legumes: Beans, lentils, and pulses are major sources of protein and fiber.

Herbs and Spices: Instead of salt, foods are flavored with natural herbs and spices. This not only adds taste but also offers health benefits.

Wine in Moderation: While this isn't a necessary component, those who choose to consume alcohol may have a small amount of wine, preferably red, with meals. Moderation is key: generally up to one glass a day for women and up to two for men.

Limiting Added Sugars: Natural sugars found in fruits and dairy are acceptable, but added sugars, found in sweets, sugary beverages, and other sweetened products, are limited.

Physical Activity: A Mediterranean lifestyle isn't only about food. Regular physical activity is crucial for overall health.

Shared Meals: One of the key, yet often overlooked components is the emphasis on enjoying meals with family and friends. This fosters a sense of community and has psychological benefits.

How does the Mediterranean diet affect people's health?

• **Cardiovascular Health**

Reduction in Heart Disease Risk: The diet emphasizes the intake of monounsaturated fats (mainly from olive oil) and omega-3 fatty acids (from fish and nuts). These fats have been linked to reducing overall cholesterol levels, decreasing inflammation, and improving heart health.

Decreased Risk of Stroke: High intake of fruits, vegetables, and whole grains, which are rich in antioxidants and dietary fiber, can help in reducing the risk of stroke.

Blood Pressure Control*: The potassium-rich fruits and vegetables in the diet can help lower blood pressure.

• **Weight Management**

Consuming whole foods with a high fiber content can promote a feeling of fullness and reduce overall calorie intake, aiding in weight management.

The balance of proteins, healthy fats, and complex carbohydrates can stabilize blood sugar levels, reducing the desire for frequent snacking.

• Diabetes Prevention and Control

The diet can reduce the risk of developing type 2 diabetes due to its emphasis on whole grains, dietary fiber, and healthy fats, which can improve insulin sensitivity.

For those with diabetes, it can help in better glycemic control.

• Cancer Prevention

The diet is rich in antioxidants and anti-inflammatory compounds found in fruits, vegetables, olive oil, and fish. These can reduce oxidative stress and inflammation, factors that contribute to cancer development.

Specific components like lycopene in tomatoes and saponins in beans have been studied for their potential anti-cancer properties.

• Cognitive Health

Some studies suggest that adherence to the Mediterranean diet can reduce the risk of neurodegenerative diseases like Alzheimer's and Parkinson's.

The antioxidants and anti-inflammatory compounds in the diet may play a role in protecting brain health.

• Mood and Mental Health

The diet can potentially play a role in reducing the risk of depression. Omega-3 fatty acids, for example, have anti-inflammatory properties and may influence neurotransmitter activity positively.

The social aspect of shared meals, a feature of Mediterranean culture, can also contribute to improved mood and mental well-being.

• Bone and Muscle Health

With an ample supply of calcium from dairy products and a variety of other essential nutrients from the whole foods in the diet, bone health can be supported.

Omega-3 fatty acids can also contribute to reducing muscle mass loss with age.

IV

- Gut Health

High fiber content, especially from whole grains, fruits, and vegetables, supports healthy digestion and promotes a balanced gut microbiome.

Fermented foods like yogurt introduce beneficial probiotics to the digestive system.

- Longevity

Due to the combined effects on heart health, weight management, and reduced risk of chronic diseases, many believe that the Mediterranean diet can contribute to increased lifespan.

What can the Mediterranean Diet Cookbook facilitate?

Diet Transition

If you're new to the Mediterranean diet, a cookbook can guide you through the transition, helping you understand the types of foods, cooking methods, and portion sizes typical of this diet.

Meal Planning

The cookbook can help with planning meals for the week or month, saving you time and ensuring a balanced intake of foods from the different food groups.

Recipe Variety

A wide range of recipes can keep your meals interesting and diverse, ensuring that you get a mix of all the nutrients and health benefits the diet offers. It also allows you to discover new flavors and ingredients you might not have tried before.

Understanding Portions

The cookbook can guide you on appropriate serving sizes to maintain a balanced diet.

Skill Development

Through diverse recipes, you can learn and hone various cooking techniques common in Mediterranean cuisine.

Health Management

Recipes can help manage or prevent certain health conditions such as heart disease, high cholesterol, diabetes, or high blood pressure, aligned with advice from your healthcare provider or dietitian.

Sustainable Eating Practices

The cookbook can guide you towards more sustainable and seasonal eating practices, a key aspect of the Mediterranean diet.

Family-Friendly Recipes

Many Mediterranean diet cookbooks include recipes that are family-friendly, encouraging healthy eating habits for everyone in the household.

30 Day Meal Plan

Day	Breakfast	Lunch	Dinner
1	Banana & Chia Seed Oats With Walnuts 6	Beef & Vegetable Stew 16	Roasted Celery Root With Yogurt Sauce 34
2	Breakfast Pancakes With Berry Sauce 6	Tuscan Pork Cassoulet 16	Veggie-stuffed Portabello Mushrooms 34
3	Crustless Tiropita (greek Cheese Pie) 6	Smoky Turkey Bake 16	Sweet Mustard Cabbage Hash 34
4	Breakfast Shakshuka Bake 7	Beef Kebabs With Onion And Pepper 16	Grilled Za´atar Zucchini Rounds 35
5	Anchovy & Spinach Sandwiches 7	Peach Pork Chops 17	Potato Tortilla With Leeks And Mushrooms 35
6	Tomato And Egg Scramble 7	Homemade Pizza Burgers 17	Parsley & Olive Zucchini Bake 35
7	Vegetable & Cheese Frittata 8	Aromatic Beef Stew 17	Tradicional Matchuba Green Beans 36
8	Bell Pepper & Cheese Egg Scramble 8	Greek-style Chicken With Potatoes 18	Fried Eggplant Rolls 36
9	Ricotta Muffins With Pear Glaze 8	Pork Chops In Tomato Olive Sauce 18	Fish & Chickpea Stew 36
10	Lime Watermelon Yogurt Smoothie 8	Chicken Bruschetta Burgers 18	Cauliflower Steaks With Arugula 37
11	Sumptuous Vegetable And Cheese Lavash Pizza 9	Spicy Mustard Pork Tenderloin 19	Roasted Vegetables And Chickpeas 37
12	Creamy Peach Smoothie 9	Green Veggie & Turkey 19	Greek-style Eggplants 37
13	Roasted Vegetable Panini 9	Harissa Turkey With Couscous 19	Mini Crustless Spinach Quiches 38
14	Za'atar Pizza 10	Milky Pork Stew 19	Artichoke & Bean Pot 38
15	Classic Shakshuka 10	Savory Tomato Chicken 20	Baked Beet & Leek With Dilly Yogurt 38

Day	Breakfast	Lunch	Dinner
16	Egg Bake 10	Chicken With Bell Peppers 20	Cauliflower Cakes With Goat Cheese 39
17	Eggs Florentine With Pancetta 11	Grilled Chicken Breasts With Italian Sauce 21	Brussels Sprouts Linguine 39
18	Mushroom And Caramelized Onion Musakhan 11	Cilantro Turkey Penne With Asparagus 21	Eggplant Rolls In Tomato Sauce 39
19	Sunday Pancakes In Berry Sauce 11	Greek-style Veggie & Beef In Pita 21	Roasted Vegetables 40
20	Eggplant, Spinach, And Feta Sandwiches 12	Chicken Breasts In White Sauce 22	Garlic-butter Asparagus With Parmesan 40
21	Grilled Caesar Salad Sandwiches 12	Coriander Pork Roast 22	Parmesan Asparagus With Tomatoes 40
22	Berry And Nut Parfait 12	Eggplant & Chicken Skillet 22	Homemade Vegetarian Moussaka 41
23	Berry-yogurt Smoothie 13	Parsley Eggplant Lamb 22	Creamy Cauliflower Chickpea Curry 41
24	Parmesan Oatmeal With Greens 13	Traditional Meatball Soup 23	Spinach & Lentil Stew 41
25	Yummy Lentil Stuffed Pitas 13	Drunken Lamb Bake 23	Baked Vegetable Stew 42
26	Pesto Salami & Cheese Egg Cupcakes 13	Fennel Beef Ribs 23	Mushroom Filled Zucchini Boats 42
27	Brown Rice Salad With Cheese 14	Slow Cooker Brussel Sprout & Chicken 23	Marinara Zoodles 42
28	Morning Pizza Frittata 14	Beef Filet Mignon In Mushroom Sauce 24	Feta & Zucchini Rosti Cakes 43
29	Kale-proscuitto Porridge 14	Sausage & Herb Eggs 24	Grilled Romaine Lettuce 43
30	Energy Nut Smoothie 15	Instant Pot Poached Salmon 25	Baby Kale And Cabbage Salad 43

Measurement Conversions

BASIC KITCHEN CONVERSIONS & EQUIVALENTS

DRY MEASUREMENTS CONVERSION CHART

3 TEASPOONS = 1 TABLESPOON = 1/16 CUP

6 TEASPOONS = 2 TABLESPOONS = 1/8 CUP

12 TEASPOONS = 4 TABLESPOONS = 1/4 CUP

24 TEASPOONS = 8 TABLESPOONS = 1/2 CUP

36 TEASPOONS = 12 TABLESPOONS = 3/4 CUP

48 TEASPOONS = 16 TABLESPOONS = 1 CUP

METRIC TO US COOKING CONVERSIONS

OVEN TEMPERATURES

120 °C = 250 °F

160 °C = 320 °F

180° C = 350 °F

205 °C = 400 °F

220 °C = 425 °F

LIQUID MEASUREMENTS CONVERSION CHART

8 FLUID OUNCES = 1 CUP = 1/2 PINT = 1/4 QUART

16 FLUID OUNCES = 2 CUPS = 1 PINT = 1/2 QUART

32 FLUID OUNCES = 4 CUPS = 2 PINTS = 1 QUART

 = 1/4 GALLON

128 FLUID OUNCES = 16 CUPS = 8 PINTS = 4 QUARTS = 1 GALLON

BAKING IN GRAMS

1 CUP FLOUR = 140 GRAMS

1 CUP SUGAR = 150 GRAMS

1 CUP POWDERED SUGAR = 160 GRAMS

1 CUP HEAVY CREAM = 235 GRAMS

VOLUME

1 MILLILITER = 1/5 TEASPOON

5 ML = 1 TEASPOON

15 ML = 1 TABLESPOON

240 ML = 1 CUP OR 8 FLUID OUNCES

1 LITER = 34 FL. OUNCES

WEIGHT

1 GRAM = .035 OUNCES

100 GRAMS = 3.5 OUNCES

500 GRAMS = 1.1 POUNDS

1 KILOGRAM = 35 OUNCES

US TO METRIC COOKING CONVERSIONS

1/5 TSP = 1 ML

1 TSP = 5 ML

1 TBSP = 15 ML

1 FL OUNCE = 30 ML

1 CUP = 237 ML

1 PINT (2 CUPS) = 473 ML

1 QUART (4 CUPS) = .95 LITER

1 GALLON (16 CUPS) = 3.8 LITERS

1 OZ = 28 GRAMS

1 POUND = 454 GRAMS

BUTTER

1 CUP BUTTER = 2 STICKS = 8 OUNCES = 230 GRAMS = 8 TABLESPOONS

WHAT DOES 1 CUP EQUAL

1 CUP = 8 FLUID OUNCES

1 CUP = 16 TABLESPOONS

1 CUP = 48 TEASPOONS

1 CUP = 1/2 PINT

1 CUP = 1/4 QUART

1 CUP = 1/16 GALLON

1 CUP = 240 ML

BAKING PAN CONVERSIONS

1 CUP ALL-PURPOSE FLOUR = 4.5 OZ

1 CUP ROLLED OATS = 3 OZ 1 LARGE EGG = 1.7 OZ

1 CUP BUTTER = 8 OZ 1 CUP MILK = 8 OZ

1 CUP HEAVY CREAM = 8.4 OZ

1 CUP GRANULATED SUGAR = 7.1 OZ

1 CUP PACKED BROWN SUGAR = 7.75 OZ

1 CUP VEGETABLE OIL = 7.7 OZ

1 CUP UNSIFTED POWDERED SUGAR = 4.4 OZ

BAKING PAN CONVERSIONS

9-INCH ROUND CAKE PAN = 12 CUPS

10-INCH TUBE PAN =16 CUPS

11-INCH BUNDT PAN = 12 CUPS

9-INCH SPRINGFORM PAN = 10 CUPS

9 X 5 INCH LOAF PAN = 8 CUPS

9-INCH SQUARE PAN = 8 CUPS

Breakfast Recipes

Banana & Chia Seed Oats With Walnuts

Servings:2

Cooking Time:15 Minutes

Ingredients:

- ½ cup walnuts, chopped
- 1 banana, peeled and sliced
- 1 cup Greek yogurt
- 2 dates, pitted and chopped
- 1 cup rolled oats
- 2 tbsp chia seeds

Directions:

1. Place banana, yogurt, dates, oats, and chia seeds in a bowl and blend until smooth. Let sit for 1 hour and spoon onto a bowl. Sprinkle with walnuts and serve.

Nutrition Info:

- Info Per Serving: Calories: 512;Fat: 24g;Protein: 25g;Carbs: 58g.

Breakfast Pancakes With Berry Sauce

Servings:4

Cooking Time: 10 Minutes

Ingredients:

- Pancakes:
- 1 cup almond flour
- 1 teaspoon baking powder
- ¼ teaspoon salt
- 6 tablespoon extra-virgin olive oil, divided
- 2 large eggs, beaten
- Zest and juice of 1 lemon
- ½ teaspoon vanilla extract
- Berry Sauce:
- 1 cup frozen mixed berries
- 1 tablespoon water, plus more as needed
- ½ teaspoon vanilla extract

Directions:

1. Make the Pancakes
2. In a large bowl, combine the almond flour, baking powder, and salt and stir to break up any clumps.
3. Add 4 tablespoons olive oil, beaten eggs, lemon zest and juice, and vanilla extract and stir until well mixed.

4. Heat 1 tablespoon of olive oil in a large skillet. Spoon about 2 tablespoons of batter for each pancake. Cook until bubbles begin to form, 4 to 5 minutes. Flip and cook for another 2 to 3 minutes. Repeat with the remaining 1 tablespoon of olive oil and batter.
5. Make the Berry Sauce
6. Combine the frozen berries, water, and vanilla extract in a small saucepan and heat over medium-high heat for 3 to 4 minutes until bubbly, adding more water as needed. Using the back of a spoon or fork, mash the berries and whisk until smooth.
7. Serve the pancakes with the berry sauce.

Nutrition Info:

- Info Per Serving: Calories: 275;Fat: 26.0g;Protein: 4.0g;Carbs: 8.0g.

Crustless Tiropita (greek Cheese Pie)

Servings:6

Cooking Time: 35 To 40 Minutes

Ingredients:

- 4 tablespoons extra-virgin olive oil, divided
- ½ cup whole-milk ricotta cheese
- 1¼ cups crumbled feta cheese
- 1 tablespoon chopped fresh dill
- 2 tablespoons chopped fresh mint
- ½ teaspoon lemon zest
- ¼ teaspoon freshly ground black pepper
- 2 large eggs
- ½ teaspoon baking powder

Directions:

1. Preheat the oven to 350°F. Coat the bottom and sides of a baking dish with 2 tablespoons of olive oil. Set aside.
2. Mix together the ricotta and feta cheese in a medium bowl and stir with a fork until well combined. Add the dill, mint, lemon zest, and black pepper and mix well.
3. In a separate bowl, whisk together the eggs and baking powder. Pour the whisked eggs into the bowl of cheese mixture. Blend well.
4. Slowly pour the mixture into the coated baking dish and drizzle with the remaining 2 tablespoons of olive oil.
5. Bake in the preheated oven for about 35 to 40 minutes, or until the pie is browned around the edges and cooked through.
6. Cool for 5 minutes before slicing into wedges.

Nutrition Info:

Info Per Serving: Calories: 181;Fat: 16.6g;Protein: 7.0g;Carbs: 1.8g.

Breakfast Shakshuka Bake

Servings:4
Cooking Time:25 Minutes
Ingredients:

- 2 tbsp extra-virgin olive oil
- 1 cup chopped red onion
- 1 chopped red bell pepper
- 1 cup finely diced potatoes
- 1 tsp garlic powder
- 1 can diced tomatoes
- ¼ tsp turmeric
- ¼ tsp paprika
- ¼ tsp dried oregano
- ¼ tsp ground cardamom
- 4 large eggs
- ¼ cup chopped fresh cilantro

Directions:

1. Preheat oven to 350 F. Warn the olive oil in a skillet over medium heat and sauté the shallots for about 3 minutes, until fragrant. Add bell peppers, potatoes, oregano, and garlic powder. Cook for 10 minutes, stirring often.
2. Pour in the tomatoes, turmeric, paprika, and cardamom and mix well until bubbly. Heat off. With a wooden spoon, make 4 holes in the mixture and crack the eggs into each space.
3. Put the skillet in the oven and cook for an additional 5-10 minutes until the whites are set, but the yolk is still runny. Sprinkle with the cilantro and serve.

Nutrition Info:

- Info Per Serving: Calories: 224;Fat: 12g;Protein: 9g;Carbs: 19.7g.

Anchovy & Spinach Sandwiches

Servings:2
Cooking Time:5 Minutes
Ingredients:

- 1 avocado, mashed
- 4 anchovies, drained
- 4 whole-wheat bread slices
- 1 cup baby spinach
- 1 tomato, sliced

Directions:

1. Spread the slices of bread with avocado mash and arrange the anchovies over. Top with baby spinach and tomato slices.

Nutrition Info:

- Info Per Serving: Calories: 300;Fat: 12g;Protein: 5g;Carbs: 10g.

Tomato And Egg Scramble

Servings:4
Cooking Time: 20 Minutes
Ingredients:

- 2 tablespoons extra-virgin olive oil
- ¼ cup finely minced red onion
- 1½ cups chopped fresh tomatoes
- 2 garlic cloves, minced
- ½ teaspoon dried thyme
- ½ teaspoon dried oregano
- 8 large eggs
- ½ teaspoon salt
- ¼ teaspoon freshly ground black pepper
- ¾ cup crumbled feta cheese
- ¼ cup chopped fresh mint leaves

Directions:

1. Heat the olive oil in a large skillet over medium heat.
2. Sauté the red onion and tomatoes in the hot skillet for 10 to 12 minutes, or until the tomatoes are softened.
3. Stir in the garlic, thyme, and oregano and sauté for 2 to 4 minutes, or until the garlic is fragrant.
4. Meanwhile, beat the eggs with the salt and pepper in a medium bowl until frothy.
5. Pour the beaten eggs into the skillet and reduce the heat to low. Scramble
6. for 3 to 4 minutes, stirring constantly, or until the eggs are set.
7. Remove from the heat and scatter with the feta cheese and mint. Serve warm.

Nutrition Info:

- Info Per Serving: Calories: 260;Fat: 21.9g;Protein: 10.2g;Carbs: 5.8g.

Vegetable & Cheese Frittata

Servings:4

Cooking Time:30 Minutes

Ingredients:

- 2 tbsp olive oil
- ½ lb cauliflower florets
- ½ cup skimmed milk
- 6 eggs
- 1 red bell pepper, chopped
- ½ cup fontina cheese, grated
- ½ tsp red pepper
- ½ tsp turmeric
- Salt and black pepper to taste

Directions:

1. Preheat oven to 360 F. In a bowl, beat the eggs with milk. Add in fontina cheese, red pepper, turmeric, salt, and pepper. Mix in red bell pepper. Warm olive oil in a skillet over medium heat, pour in the egg mixture and cook for 4-5 minutes. Set aside.

2. Blanch the cauliflower florets in a pot for 5 minutes until tender. Spread over the egg mixture. Place the skillet in the oven and bake for 15 minutes or until golden brown. Allow cooling for a few minutes before slicing. Serve warm.

Nutrition Info:

- Info Per Serving: Calories: 312;Fat: 18g;Protein: 21g;Carbs: 17g.

Bell Pepper & Cheese Egg Scramble

Servings:4

Cooking Time:20 Minutes

Ingredients:

- ½ cup fresh mozzarella cheese, crumbled
- 2 tsp olive oil
- 1 cup bell peppers, chopped
- 2 garlic cloves, minced
- 6 large eggs, beaten
- Salt to taste
- 2 tbsp fresh cilantro, chopped

Directions:

1. Warm the olive oil in a large skillet over medium heat. Add the peppers and sauté for 5 minutes, stirring occasionally. Add the garlic and cook for 1 minute. Stir in the eggs and salt and cook for 2-3 minutes until the eggs begin to set on the bottom. Top with mozzarella cheese and cook the eggs for about 2 more minutes, stirring slowly, until the eggs are soft-set and custardy. Sprinkle with cilantro and serve.

Nutrition Info:

- Info Per Serving: Calories: 259;Fat: 16g;Protein: 29g;Carbs: 2g.

Ricotta Muffins With Pear Glaze

Servings:4

Cooking Time:42 Minutes

Ingredients:

- 16 oz ricotta cheese
- 2 large eggs
- ¼ cup flour
- 1 tbsp sugar
- 1 tsp vanilla extract
- ¼ tsp ground nutmeg
- 1 pear, cored and diced
- 1 tbsp sugar

Directions:

1. Preheat the oven to 400 F. In a large bowl, whisk the ricotta, eggs, flour, sugar, vanilla, and nutmeg. Spoon into 4 greased ramekins. Bake for 20-25 minutes. Transfer to a wire rack to cool before unmolding.

2. Place the pear, sugar, and 2 tbsp of water in a small saucepan over low heat. Simmer for 10 minutes until slightly softened. Remove from the heat, and stir in the honey. Serve the ricotta ramekins glazed with pear sauce.

Nutrition Info:

- Info Per Serving: Calories: 329;Fat: 19g;Protein: 17g;Carbs: 23g.

Lime Watermelon Yogurt Smoothie

Servings:6

Cooking Time:5 Minutes

Ingredients:

- ½ cup almond milk
- 2 cups watermelon, cubed
- ½ cup Greek yogurt
- ½ tsp lime zest

Directions:

1. In a food processor, blend watermelon, almond milk, lime zest, and yogurt until smooth. Serve into glasses.

Nutrition Info:

- Info Per Serving: Calories: 260;Fat: 10g;Protein: 2g;Carbs: 6g.

Sumptuous Vegetable And Cheese Lavash Pizza

Servings:4
Cooking Time: 11 Minutes
Ingredients:

- 2 lavash breads
- 2 tablespoons extra-virgin olive oil
- 10 ounces frozen spinach, thawed and squeezed dry
- 1 cup shredded fontina cheese
- 1 tomato, cored and cut into ½-inch pieces
- ½ cup pitted large green olives, chopped
- ¼ teaspoon red pepper flakes
- 3 garlic cloves, minced
- ¼ teaspoon sea salt
- ¼ teaspoon ground black pepper
- ½ cup grated Parmesan cheese

Directions:
1. Preheat oven to 475ºF.
2. Brush the lavash breads with olive oil, then place them on two baking sheet. Heat in the preheated oven for 4 minutes or until lightly browned. Flip the breads halfway through the cooking time.
3. Meanwhile, combine the spinach, fontina cheese, tomato pieces, olives, red pepper flakes, garlic, salt, and black pepper in a large bowl. Stir to mix well.
4. Remove the lavash bread from the oven and sit them on two large plates, spread them with the spinach mixture, then scatter with the Parmesan cheese on top.
5. Bake in the oven for 7 minutes or until the cheese melts and well browned.
6. Slice and serve warm.

Nutrition Info:
- Info Per Serving: Calories: 431;Fat: 21.5g;Protein: 20.0g;Carbs: 38.4g.

Creamy Peach Smoothie

Servings:2
Cooking Time: 0 Minutes
Ingredients:

- 2 cups packed frozen peaches, partially thawed
- ½ ripe avocado
- ½ cup plain or vanilla Greek yogurt
- 2 tablespoons flax meal
- 1 tablespoon honey
- 1 teaspoon orange extract
- 1 teaspoon vanilla extract

Directions:
1. Place all the ingredients in a blender and blend until completely mixed and smooth.
2. Divide the mixture into two bowls and serve immediately.

Nutrition Info:
- Info Per Serving: Calories: 212;Fat: 13.1g;Protein: 6.0g;Carbs: 22.5g.

Roasted Vegetable Panini

Servings:4
Cooking Time: 15 Minutes
Ingredients:

- 2 tablespoons extra-virgin olive oil, divided
- 1½ cups diced broccoli
- 1 cup diced zucchini
- ¼ cup diced onion
- ¼ teaspoon dried oregano
- ⅛ teaspoon kosher or sea salt
- ⅛ teaspoon freshly ground black pepper
- 1 jar roasted red peppers, drained and finely chopped
- 2 tablespoons grated Parmesan or Asiago cheese
- 1 cup fresh Mozzarella, sliced
- 1 whole-grain Italian loaf, cut into 4 equal lengths
- Cooking spray

Directions:
1. Place a large, rimmed baking sheet in the oven. Preheat the oven to 450ºF with the baking sheet inside.
2. In a large bowl, stir together 1 tablespoon of the oil, broccoli, zucchini, onion, oregano, salt and pepper.
3. Remove the baking sheet from the oven and spritz the baking sheet with cooking spray. Spread the vegetable mixture on the baking sheet and roast for 5 minutes, stirring once halfway through cooking.
4. Remove the baking sheet from the oven. Stir in the red peppers and Parmesan cheese.
5. In a large skillet over medium-high heat, heat the remaining 1 tablespoon of the oil.
6. Cut open each section of bread horizontally, but don't cut all the way through. Fill each with the vegetable mix (about ½ cup), and layer 1 ounce of sliced Mozzarella cheese on top. Close the sandwiches, and place two of them on the skillet. Place a heavy object on top and grill for 2½ minutes. Flip the sandwiches and grill for another 2½ minutes.
7. Repeat the grilling process with the remaining two sandwiches.
8. Serve hot.

Nutrition Info:

- Info Per Serving: Calories: 116;Fat: 4.0g;Protein: 12.0g;Carbs: 9.0g.

Za'atar Pizza

Servings:4

Cooking Time: 1o To 12 Minutes

Ingredients:

- 1 sheet puff pastry
- ¼ cup extra-virgin olive oil
- ⅓ cup za'atar seasoning

Directions:

1. Preheat the oven to 350ºF. Line a baking sheet with parchment paper.

2. Place the puff pastry on the prepared baking sheet. Cut the pastry into desired slices.

3. Brush the pastry with the olive oil. Sprinkle with the za'atar seasoning.

4. Put the pastry in the oven and bake for 10 to 12 minutes, or until edges are lightly browned and puffed up.

5. Serve warm.

Nutrition Info:

- Info Per Serving: Calories: 374;Fat: 30.0g;Protein: 3.0g;Carbs: 20.0g.

Classic Shakshuka

Servings:2

Cooking Time: 30 Minutes

Ingredients:

- 1 tablespoon olive oil
- ½ red pepper, diced
- ½ medium onion, diced
- 2 small garlic cloves, minced
- ½ teaspoon smoked paprika
- ½ teaspoon cumin
- Pinch red pepper flakes
- 1 can fire-roasted tomatoes
- ¼ teaspoon salt
- Pinch freshly ground black pepper
- 1 ounce crumbled feta cheese (about ¼ cup)
- 3 large eggs
- 3 tablespoons minced fresh parsley

Directions:

1. Heat the olive oil in a skillet over medium-high heat and add the pepper, onion, and garlic. Sauté until the vegetables start to turn golden.

2. Add the paprika, cumin, and red pepper flakes and stir to toast the spices for about 30 seconds. Add the tomatoes with their juices.

3. Reduce the heat and let the sauce simmer for 10 minutes, or until it starts to thicken. Add the salt and pepper. Taste the sauce and adjust seasonings as necessary.

4. Scatter the feta cheese on top. Make 3 wells in the sauce and crack one egg into each well.

5. Cover and let the eggs cook for about 7 minutes. Remove the lid and continue cooking for 5 minutes more, or until the yolks are cooked to desired doneness.

6. Garnish with fresh parsley and serve.

Nutrition Info:

- Info Per Serving: Calories: 289;Fat: 18.2g;Protein: 15.1g;Carbs: 18.5g.

Egg Bake

Servings:2

Cooking Time: 30 Minutes

Ingredients:

- 1 tablespoon olive oil
- 1 slice whole-grain bread
- 4 large eggs
- 3 tablespoons unsweetened almond milk
- ½ teaspoon onion powder
- ¼ teaspoon garlic powder
- ¾ cup chopped cherry tomatoes
- ¼ teaspoon salt
- Pinch freshly ground black pepper

Directions:

1. Preheat the oven to 375ºF.

2. Coat two ramekins with the olive oil and transfer to a baking sheet. Line the bottom of each ramekin with ½ of bread slice.

3. In a medium bowl, whisk together the eggs, almond milk, onion powder, garlic powder, tomatoes, salt, and pepper until well combined.

4. Pour the mixture evenly into two ramekins. Bake in the preheated oven for 30 minutes, or until the eggs are completely set.

5. Cool for 5 minutes before serving.

Nutrition Info:

- Info Per Serving: Calories: 240;Fat: 17.4g;Protein: 9.0g;Carbs: 12.2g.

Mushroom And Caramelized Onion Musakhan

Servings:4

Cooking Time: 1 Hour 5 Minutes

Ingredients:

- 2 tablespoons sumac, plus more for sprinkling
- 1 teaspoon ground allspice
- ½ teaspoon ground cardamom
- ½ teaspoon ground cumin
- 3 tablespoons extra-virgin olive oil, divided
- 2 pounds portobello mushroom caps, gills removed, caps halved and sliced ½ inch thick
- 3 medium white onions, coarsely chopped
- ¼ cup water
- Kosher salt, to taste
- 1 whole-wheat Turkish flatbread
- ¼ cup pine nuts
- 1 lemon, wedged

Directions:

1. Preheat the oven to 350ºF.

2. Combine 2 tablespoons of sumac, allspice, cardamom, and cumin in a small bowl. Stir to mix well.

3. Heat 2 tablespoons of olive oil in an oven-proof skillet over medium-high heat until shimmering.

4. Add the mushroom to the skillet and sprinkle with half of sumac mixture. Sauté for 8 minutes or until the mushrooms are tender. You may need to work in batches to avoid overcrowding. Transfer the mushrooms to a plate and set side.

5. Heat 1 tablespoon of olive oil in the skillet over medium-high heat until shimmering.

6. Add the onion and sauté for 20 minutes or until caramelized. Sprinkle with remaining sumac mixture, then cook for 1 more minute.

7. Pour in the water and sprinkle with salt. Bring to a simmer.

8. Turn off the heat and put the mushroom back to the skillet.

9. Place the skillet in the preheated oven and bake for 30 minutes.

10. Remove the skillet from the oven and let the mushroom sit for 10 minutes until cooled down.

11. Heat the Turkish flatbread in a baking dish in the oven for 5 minutes or until warmed through.

12. Arrange the bread on a large plate and top with mushrooms, onions, and roasted pine nuts. Squeeze the lemon wedges over and sprinkle with more sumac. Serve immediately.

Nutrition Info:

- Info Per Serving: Calories: 336;Fat: 18.7g;Protein: 11.5g;Carbs: 34.3g.

Eggs Florentine With Pancetta

Servings:2

Cooking Time:20 Minutes

Ingredients:

- 1 English muffin, toasted and halved
- ¼ cup chopped pancetta
- 2 tsp hollandaise sauce
- 1 cup spinach
- Salt and black pepper to taste
- 2 large eggs

Directions:

1. Place pancetta in a pan over medium heat and cook for 5 minutes until crispy; reserve. Add the baby spinach and cook for 2-3 minutes in the same pan until the spinach wilts. Fill a pot with 3 inches of water over medium heat and bring to a boil. Add 1 tbsp of vinegar and reduce the heat.

2. Crack the eggs one at a time into a small dish and gently pour into the simmering water. Poach the eggs for 2-3 minutes until the whites are set, but the yolks are still soft; remove with a slotted spoon. Divide the spinach between muffin halves and top with pancetta and poached eggs. Spoon the hollandaise sauce on top and serve.

Nutrition Info:

- Info Per Serving: Calories: 173;Fat: 7g;Protein: 11g;Carbs: 17g.

Sunday Pancakes In Berry Sauce

Servings:4

Cooking Time:20 Minutes

Ingredients:

- Pancakes
- 6 tbsp olive oil
- 1 cup flour
- 1 tsp baking powder
- ¼ tsp salt
- 2 large eggs
- 1 lemon, zested and juiced
- ½ tsp vanilla extract
- ½ tsp dark rum
- Berry Sauce
- 1 cup mixed berries

- 3 tbsp sugar
- 1 tbsp lemon juice
- ½ tsp vanilla extract

Directions:

1.   In a large bowl, combine the flour, baking powder, and salt and whisk to break up any clumps. Add 4 tablespoons of olive oil, eggs, lemon zest and juice, rum, and vanilla extract and whisk to combine well. Brush a frying pan with butter over medium heat and cook the pancakes for 5-7 minutes, flipping once until bubbles begin to form.

2.   To make the sauce, pour the mixed berries, lemon juice, vanilla, and sugar in a small saucepan over medium heat. Cook for 3-4 minutes until bubbly, adding a little water if the mixture is too thick. Mash the berries with a fork and stir until smooth. Pour over the pancakes and serve.

Nutrition Info:

- Info Per Serving: Calories: 275;Fat: 26g;Protein: 4g;Carbs: 8g.

Eggplant, Spinach, And Feta Sandwiches

Servings:2
Cooking Time: 6 To 8 Minutes

Ingredients:

- 1 medium eggplant, sliced into ½-inch-thick slices
- 2 tablespoons olive oil
- Sea salt and freshly ground pepper, to taste
- 5 to 6 tablespoons hummus
- 4 slices whole-wheat bread, toasted
- 1 cup baby spinach leaves
- 2 ounces feta cheese, softened

Directions:

1.   Preheat the grill to medium-high heat.

2.   Salt both sides of the sliced eggplant, and let sit for 20 minutes to draw out the bitter juices.

3.   Rinse the eggplant and pat dry with a paper towel.

4.   Brush the eggplant slices with olive oil and season with sea salt and freshly ground pepper to taste.

5.   Grill the eggplant until lightly charred on both sides but still slightly firm in the middle, about 3 to 4 minutes per side.

6.   Spread the hummus on the bread slices and top with the spinach leaves, feta cheese, and grilled eggplant. Top with the other slice of bread and serve immediately.

Nutrition Info:

- Info Per Serving: Calories: 493;Fat: 25.3g;Protein: 17.1g;Carbs: 50.9g.

Grilled Caesar Salad Sandwiches

Servings:2
Cooking Time: 5 Minutes

Ingredients:

- ¾ cup olive oil, divided
- 2 romaine lettuce hearts, left intact
- 3 to 4 anchovy fillets
- Juice of 1 lemon
- 2 to 3 cloves garlic, peeled
- 1 teaspoon Dijon mustard
- ¼ teaspoon Worcestershire sauce
- Sea salt and freshly ground pepper, to taste
- 2 slices whole-wheat bread, toasted
- Freshly grated Parmesan cheese, for serving

Directions:

1.   Preheat the grill to medium-high heat and oil the grates.

2.   On a cutting board, drizzle the lettuce with 1 to 2 tablespoons of olive oil and place on the grates.

3.   Grill for 5 minutes, turning until lettuce is slightly charred on all sides. Let lettuce cool enough to handle.

4.   In a food processor, combine the remaining olive oil with the anchovies, lemon juice, garlic, mustard, and Worcestershire sauce.

5.   Pulse the ingredients until you have a smooth emulsion. Season with sea salt and freshly ground pepper to taste. Chop the lettuce in half and place on the bread.

6.   Drizzle with the dressing and serve with a sprinkle of Parmesan cheese.

Nutrition Info:

- Info Per Serving: Calories: 949;Fat: 85.6g;Protein: 12.9g;Carbs: 34.1g.

Berry And Nut Parfait

Servings:2
Cooking Time: 0 Minutes

Ingredients:

- 2 cups plain Greek yogurt
- 2 tablespoons honey
- 1 cup fresh raspberries
- 1 cup fresh blueberries
- ½ cup walnut pieces

Directions:

1.   In a medium bowl, whisk the yogurt and honey. Spoon into 2 serving bowls.

2.   Top each with ½ cup blueberries, ½ cup raspberries, and ¼ cup walnut pieces. Serve immediately.

Nutrition Info:

6. Stir well and season with salt and black pepper to taste. Serve warm.

Nutrition Info:

- Info Per Serving: Calories: 257;Fat: 14.0g;Protein: 12.2g;Carbs: 30.2g.

Berry-yogurt Smoothie

Servings:1
Cooking Time:5 Minutes
Ingredients:

- ½ cup Greek yogurt
- ¼ cup milk
- ½ cup fresh blueberries
- 1 tsp vanilla sugar
- 2 ice cubes

Directions:

1. Pulse the Greek yogurt, milk, vanilla sugar, and berries in your blender until the berries are liquefied. Add the ice cubes and blend on high until thick and smooth. Serve.

Nutrition Info:

- Info Per Serving: Calories: 230;Fat: 8.8g;Protein: 16g;Carbs: 23g.

Parmesan Oatmeal With Greens

Servings:2
Cooking Time: 18 Minutes
Ingredients:

- 1 tablespoon olive oil
- ¼ cup minced onion
- 2 cups greens (arugula, baby spinach, chopped kale, or Swiss chard)
- ¾ cup gluten-free old-fashioned oats
- 1½ cups water, or low-sodium chicken stock
- 2 tablespoons Parmesan cheese
- Salt, to taste
- Pinch freshly ground black pepper

Directions:

1. Heat the olive oil in a saucepan over medium-high heat. Add the minced onion and sauté for 2 minutes, or until softened.

2. Add the greens and stir until they begin to wilt. Transfer this mixture to a bowl and set aside.

3. Add the oats to the pan and let them toast for about 2 minutes. Add the water and bring the oats to a boil.

4. Reduce the heat to low, cover, and let the oats cook for 10 minutes, or until the liquid is absorbed and the oats are tender.

5. Stir the Parmesan cheese into the oats, and add the onion and greens back to the pan. Add additional water if needed, so the oats are creamy and not dry.

Yummy Lentil Stuffed Pitas

Servings:4
Cooking Time:20 Minutes
Ingredients:

- 4 pitta breads, halved horizontally
- 2 tbsp olive oil
- 1 tomato, cubed
- 1 red onion, chopped
- 1 garlic clove, minced
- ¼ cup parsley, chopped
- 1 cup lentils, rinsed
- ¼ cup lemon juice
- Salt and black pepper to taste

Directions:

1. Bring a pot of salted water to a boil over high heat. Pour in the lentils and lower the heat. Cover and let it simmer for 15 minutes or until lentils are tender, adding more water if needed. Drain and set aside.

2. Warm the olive oil in a skillet over medium heat and cook the onion and garlic and for 3 minutes until soft and translucent. Stir in tomato, lemon juice, salt, and pepper and cook for another 10 minutes. Add the lentils and parsley to the skillet and stir to combine. Fill the pita bread with the lentil mixture. Roll up and serve immediately. Enjoy!

Nutrition Info:

- Info Per Serving: Calories: 390;Fat: 2g;Protein: 29g;Carbs: 68g.

Pesto Salami & Cheese Egg Cupcakes

Servings:6
Cooking Time:25 Minutes
Ingredients:

- ½ cup roasted red peppers, chopped
- 1 tbsp olive oil
- 5 eggs, whisked
- 4 oz Italian dry salami, sliced
- 1/3 cup spinach, chopped
- ¼ cup ricotta cheese, crumbled
- Salt and black pepper to taste
- 1 ½ tbsp basil pesto

Directions:

1. Preheat the oven to 380 F. Brush 6 ramekin cups with olive oil and line them with dry salami slices. Top with spinach, ricotta cheese, and roasted peppers. Whisk the eggs with pesto, salt, and pepper in a bowl and pour over the peppers. Bake for 15 minutes and serve warm.

Nutrition Info:

- Info Per Serving: Calories: 120;Fat: 8g;Protein: 10g;Carbs: 2g.

Brown Rice Salad With Cheese

Servings:4
Cooking Time:10 Minutes
Ingredients:

- 2 tbsp olive oil
- ½ cup brown rice
- 1 lb watercress
- 1 Roma tomato, sliced
- 4 oz feta cheese, crumbled
- 2 tbsp fresh basil, chopped
- Salt and black pepper to taste
- 2 tbsp lemon juice
- ¼ tsp lemon zest

Directions:

1. Bring to a boil salted water in a pot over medium heat. Add in the rice and cook for 15-18 minutes. Drain and let cool completely. Whisk the olive oil, lemon zest, lemon juice, salt, and pepper in a salad bowl. Add in the watercress, cooled rice, and basil and toss to coat. Top with feta cheese and tomato. Serve immediately.

Nutrition Info:

- Info Per Serving: Calories: 480;Fat: 24g;Protein: 14g;Carbs: 55g.

Morning Pizza Frittata

Servings:4
Cooking Time:20 Minutes
Ingredients:

- 2 tbsp butter
- 8 oz pancetta, chopped
- ½ onion, finely chopped
- 1 cup mushrooms, sliced
- 8 large eggs, beaten
- ¼ cup heavy cream
- 1 tsp dried oregano
- ¼ tsp red pepper flakes
- ½ cup mozzarella, shredded
- 8 cherry tomatoes, halved

- 4 black olives, sliced

Directions:

1. Melt the butter in a large skillet over medium heat until. Add the pancetta and cook for 4 minutes until browned. Stir in the onion and mushrooms and cook for 3 more minutes, stirring occasionally, until the veggies are tender. In a bowl, beat the eggs, heavy cream, oregano, and red pepper flakes.

2. Pour over the veggies and pancetta. Cook for about 5-6 minutes until the eggs are set. Spread the mozzarella cheese all over and arrange the cherry tomatoes on top. Place under the preheated broiler for 4-5 minutes. Leave to cool slightly and cut into wedges. Top with sliced olives and serve warm.

Nutrition Info:

- Info Per Serving: Calories: 595;Fat: 43g;Protein: 38g;Carbs: 14g.

Kale-proscuitto Porridge

Servings:2
Cooking Time:30 Minutes
Ingredients:

- 1 tbsp olive oil
- 1 green onion, chopped
- 1 oz prosciutto, chopped
- 2 cups kale
- ¾ cup old-fashioned oats
- 2 tbsp Parmesan, grated
- Salt and black pepper to taste

Directions:

1. Warm the olive oil in a pan over medium heat. Sauté the onion and prosciutto and sauté for 4 minutes or until the prosciutto is crisp and the onion turns golden. Add the kale and stir for 5 minutes until wilted. Transfer to a bowl.

2. Add the oats to the pan and let them toast for 2 minutes. Add 1 ½ of water or chicken stock and bring to a boil. Reduce the heat to low, cover, and let the oats simmer for 10 minutes or until the liquid is absorbed and the oats are tender.

3. Stir in Parmesan cheese, and add the onions, prosciutto, and kale back to the pan and cook until creamy but not dry. Adjust the seasoning with salt and pepper and serve.

Nutrition Info:

- Info Per Serving: Calories: 258;Fat: 12g;Protein: 11g;Carbs: 29g.

Energy Nut Smoothie

Servings:1
Cooking Time:10 Minutes
Ingredients:

- 1 tbsp extra-virgin olive oil
- ½ cup Greek yogurt
- ½ cup almond milk
- ½ orange, zested and juiced
- 1 tbsp pistachios, chopped
- 1 tsp honey
- ½ tsp ground allspice
- ¼ tsp ground cinnamon
- ¼ tsp vanilla extract

Directions:

1. Place the yogurt, almond milk, orange zest and juice, olive oil, pistachios, honey, allspice, cinnamon, and vanilla in a blender and pulse until smooth and creamy. Add a little water to achieve your desired consistency. Serve in a chilled glass.

Nutrition Info:

- Info Per Serving: Calories: 264;Fat: 22.2g;Protein: 6g;Carbs: 12g.

Poultry And Meats Recipes

Beef & Vegetable Stew

Servings:6
Cooking Time:and Total Time: 35 Minutes
Ingredients:

- 2 sweet potatoes, cut into chunks
- 2 lb beef meat for stew
- ¾ cup red wine
- 1 tbsp butter
- 6 oz tomato paste
- 6 oz baby carrots, chopped
- 1 onion, finely chopped
- Salt to taste
- 4 cups beef broth
- ½ cup green peas
- 1 tsp dried thyme
- 3 garlic cloves, crushed

Directions:

1. Heat the butter on Sauté in your Instant pot. Add beef and brown for 5-6 minutes. Add onions and garlic, and keep stirring for 3 more minutes. Add the remaining ingredients and seal the lid. Cook on Meat/Stew for 20 minutes on High pressure. Do a quick release and serve immediately.

Nutrition Info:

- Info Per Serving: Calories: 470;Fat: 15g;Protein: 51g;Carbs: 27g.

Tuscan Pork Cassoulet

Servings:4
Cooking Time:30 Minutes
Ingredients:

- 2 tbsp olive oil
- 2 lb pork loin, sliced
- 4 garlic cloves, minced
- 1 cup green olives, halved
- 1 tbsp capers
- ½ cup tomato puree
- Salt and black pepper to taste
- 2 tbsp parsley, chopped
- Juice of 1 lime

Directions:

1. Warm the olive oil in a skillet over medium heat and cook garlic and pork for 5 minutes. Stir in green olives, capers, tomato purée, salt, pepper, parsley, and lime juice and bring to a simmer. Cook for another 15 minutes. Serve.

Nutrition Info:

- Info Per Serving: Calories: 260;Fat: 13g;Protein: 14g;Carbs: 22g.

Smoky Turkey Bake

Servings:4
Cooking Time:50 Minutes
Ingredients:

- 1 skinless, boneless turkey breast, roughly cubed
- 2 tbsp olive oil
- 1 shallot, sliced
- 1 tbsp smoked paprika
- 2 chili peppers, chopped
- Salt and black pepper to taste
- ½ cup chicken stock
- 1 tbsp parsley, chopped

Directions:

1. Preheat the oven to 390 F. Grease a roasting pan with oil. Toss turkey, shallot, paprika, chili peppers, salt, pepper, stock, and parsley on the pan and bake for 40 minutes. Serve.

Nutrition Info:

- Info Per Serving: Calories: 320;Fat: 19g;Protein: 35g;Carbs: 24g.

Beef Kebabs With Onion And Pepper

Servings:6
Cooking Time: 10 Minutes
Ingredients:

- 2 pounds beef fillet
- 1½ teaspoons salt
- 1 teaspoon freshly ground black pepper
- ½ teaspoon ground nutmeg
- ½ teaspoon ground allspice
- ⅓ cup extra-virgin olive oil
- 1 large onion, cut into 8 quarters
- 1 large red bell pepper, cut into 1-inch cubes

Directions:

1. Preheat the grill to high heat.

2. Cut the beef into 1-inch cubes and put them in a large bowl.

3. In a small bowl, mix together the salt, black pepper, allspice, and nutmeg.

4. Pour the olive oil over the beef and toss to coat. Evenly sprinkle the seasoning over the beef and toss to coat all pieces.

5. Skewer the beef, alternating every 1 or 2 pieces with a piece of onion or bell pepper.

6. To cook, place the skewers on the preheated grill, and flip every 2 to 3 minutes until all sides have cooked to desired doneness, 6 minutes for medium-rare, 8 minutes for well done. Serve hot.

Nutrition Info:

- Info Per Serving: Calories: 485;Fat: 36.0g;Protein: 35.0g;Carbs: 4.0g.

Peach Pork Chops

Servings:4
Cooking Time:30 Minutes
Ingredients:

- 2 tbsp olive oil
- ½ tsp cayenne powder
- 4 pork chops, boneless
- ¼ cup peach preserves
- 1 tbsp thyme, chopped

Directions:

1. In a bowl, mix peach preserves, olive oil, and cayenne powder. Preheat your grill to medium. Rub pork chops with some peach glaze and grill for 10 minutes. Turn the chops, rub more glaze and cook for 10 minutes. Top with thyme.

Nutrition Info:

- Info Per Serving: Calories: 240;Fat: 12g;Protein: 24g;Carbs: 7g.

Homemade Pizza Burgers

Servings:4
Cooking Time:20 Minutes
Ingredients:

- ¼ tsp mustard powder
- ¼ tsp cumin
- 1 ¼ lb ground beef
- ½ tsp garlic salt
- ¼ tsp red pepper flakes
- ½ tsp Italian seasoning
- 1 cup passata
- 8 mozzarella cheese slices

Directions:

1. Preheat your grill to medium. In a large bowl, lightly mix with your hands the ground beef, mustard powder, cumin, garlic salt, pepper flakes, and Italian seasoning. Shape the mixture into 4 patties. Grill the burgers for about 10 minutes, turning them occasionally to ensure even cooking. In the last 2 minutes of cooking, top each burger with a generous tablespoon of passata and 2 slices of cheese per burger. Remove and let sit for 1–2 minutes before serving.

Nutrition Info:

- Info Per Serving: Calories: 556;Fat: 39g;Protein: 41g;Carbs: 8g.

Aromatic Beef Stew

Servings:4
Cooking Time:80 Minutes
Ingredients:

- 3 tbsp olive oil
- 2 lb beef shoulder, cubed
- Salt and black pepper to taste
- 1 onion, chopped
- 2 garlic cloves, minced
- 3 tomatoes, grated
- 1 tsp red chili flakes
- 2 cups chicken stock
- 1 cup couscous
- 10 green olives, sliced
- 1 tbsp cilantro, chopped

Directions:

1. Warm the olive oil in a pot over medium heat and cook beef for 5 minutes until brown, stirring often. Add in onion and garlic and cook for another 5 minutes. Stir in tomatoes, salt, pepper, chicken stock, olives, and red chili flakes. Bring to a boil and simmer for 1 hour. Cover the couscous with boiling water in a bowl, cover, and let sit for 4-5 minutes until the water has been absorbed. Fluff with a fork and season with salt and pepper. Pour the stew over and scatter with cilantro.

Nutrition Info:

- Info Per Serving: Calories: 420;Fat: 18g;Protein: 35g;Carbs: 26g.

Greek-style Chicken With Potatoes

Servings:4
Cooking Time:30 Minutes
Ingredients:
- 4 potatoes, peeled and quartered
- 4 boneless skinless chicken drumsticks
- 4 cups water
- 2 lemons, zested and juiced
- 1 tbsp olive oil
- 2 tsp fresh oregano
- Salt and black pepper to taste
- 2 Serrano peppers, minced
- 3 tbsp finely chopped parsley
- 1 cup packed watercress
- 1 cucumber, thinly chopped
- 10 cherry tomatoes, quartered
- 16 Kalamata olives, pitted
- ¼ cup hummus
- ¼ cup feta cheese, crumbled
- Lemon wedges, for serving

Directions:
1. Add water and potatoes to your Instant Pot. Set trivet over them. In a baking bowl, mix lemon juice, olive oil, black pepper, oregano, zest, salt, and Serrano peppers. Add chicken drumsticks in the marinade and stir to coat.
2. Set the bowl with chicken on the trivet in the cooker. Seal the lid, select Manual and cook on High for 15 minutes. Do a quick release. Take out the bowl with chicken and the trivet from the pot. Drain potatoes and add parsley and salt. Split the potatoes among serving plates and top with watercress, cucumber slices, hummus, cherry tomatoes, chicken, olives, and feta cheese. Garnish with lemon wedges. Serve.

Nutrition Info:
- Info Per Serving: Calories: 726;Fat: 15g;Protein: 72g;Carbs: 75g.

Pork Chops In Tomato Olive Sauce

Servings:4
Cooking Time:20 Minutes
Ingredients:
- 2 tbsp olive oil
- 4 pork loin chops, boneless
- 6 tomatoes, crushed
- 3 tbsp basil, chopped
- 10 black olives, halved
- 1 yellow onion, chopped
- 1 garlic clove, minced

Directions:
1. Warm the olive oil in a skillet over medium heat and brown pork chops for 6 minutes on all sides. Share into plates. In the same skillet, stir tomatoes, basil, olives, onion, and garlic and simmer for 4 minutes. Drizzle tomato sauce over.

Nutrition Info:
- Info Per Serving: Calories: 340;Fat: 18g;Protein: 35g;Carbs: 13g.

Chicken Bruschetta Burgers

Servings:2
Cooking Time: 16 Minutes
Ingredients:
- 1 tablespoon olive oil
- 2 garlic cloves, minced
- 3 tablespoons finely minced onion
- 1 teaspoon dried basil
- 3 tablespoons minced sun-dried tomatoes packed in olive oil
- 8 ounces ground chicken breast
- ¼ teaspoon salt
- 3 pieces small Mozzarella balls, minced

Directions:
1. Heat the olive oil in a nonstick skillet over medium-high heat. Add the garlic and onion and sauté for 5 minutes until tender. Stir in the basil.
2. Remove from the skillet to a medium bowl.
3. Add the tomatoes, ground chicken, and salt and stir until incorporated. Mix in the Mozzarella balls.
4. Divide the chicken mixture in half and form into two burgers, each about ¾-inch thick.
5. Heat the same skillet over medium-high heat and add the burgers. Cook each side for 5 to 6 minutes, or until they reach an internal temperature of 165ºF.
6. Serve warm.

Nutrition Info:
- Info Per Serving: Calories: 300;Fat: 17.0g;Protein: 32.2g;Carbs: 6.0g.

Spicy Mustard Pork Tenderloin

Servings:4

Cooking Time:30 Minutes

Ingredients:

- 2 tbsp olive oil
- 1 pork tenderloin
- 2 garlic cloves, minced
- ½ cup fresh parsley, chopped
- 1 tbsp rosemary, chopped
- 1 tbsp tarragon, chopped
- 3 tbsp stone-ground mustard
- ½ tsp cumin powder
- ½ chili pepper, minced
- Salt and black pepper to taste

Directions:

1. Preheat oven to 400 F. In a food processor, blend parsley, tarragon, rosemary, mustard, olive oil, chili pepper, cumin, salt, garlic, and pepper until smooth. Rub the mixture all over the pork and transfer onto a lined baking sheet. Bake in the oven for 20-25 minutes. Slice and serve.

Nutrition Info:

- Info Per Serving: Calories: 970;Fat: 29g;Protein: 16g;Carbs: 2.6g.

Green Veggie & Turkey

Servings:4

Cooking Time:40 Minutes

Ingredients:

- 3 tbsp olive oil
- 1 lb asparagus, halved
- 1 lb turkey breast, sliced
- 1 cup chicken stock
- Salt and black pepper to taste
- 1 cup canned artichoke hearts
- 2 tomatoes, chopped
- 10 Kalamata olives, sliced
- 1 shallot, chopped
- 3 garlic cloves, minced
- 3 tbsp dill, chopped

Directions:

1. Warm the olive oil in a pot over medium heat and cook turkey and garlic for 8 minutes or until the meat is golden brown. Stir in the asparagus, chopped tomatoes, chicken stock, salt, black pepper, artichoke hearts, Kalamata olives, and shallot and bring to a boil. Lower the heat and simmer for 20 minutes. Garnish with dill and serve.

Nutrition Info:

- Info Per Serving: Calories: 300;Fat: 17g;Protein: 35g;Carbs: 24g.

Harissa Turkey With Couscous

Servings:4

Cooking Time:20 Min + Marinating Time

Ingredients:

- 1 lb skinless turkey breast slices
- 2 tbsp olive oil
- 1 tsp garlic powder
- ½ tsp ground coriander
- 1 tbsp harissa seasoning
- 1 cup couscous
- 2 tbsp raisins, soaked
- 2 tbsp chopped parsley
- Salt and black pepper to taste

Directions:

1. Whisk the olive oil, garlic powder, ground coriander, harissa, salt, and pepper in a bowl. Add the turkey slices and toss to coat. Marinate covered for 30 minutes. Place the couscous in a large bowl and pour 1 ½ cups of salted boiling water. Cover and leave to sit for 5 minutes. Fluff with a fork and stir in raisins and parsley. Keep warm until ready to serve.

2. Preheat your grill to high. Place the turkey slices on the grill and cook for 3 minutes per side until cooked through with no pink showing. Serve with the couscous.

Nutrition Info:

- Info Per Serving: Calories: 350;Fat: 7g;Protein: 47g;Carbs: 19g.

Milky Pork Stew

Servings:4

Cooking Time:50 Minutes

Ingredients:

- 1 tbsp avocado oil
- 1 ½ cups buttermilk
- 1 ½ lb pork meat, cubed
- 1 red onion, chopped
- 1 garlic clove, minced
- ½ cup chicken stock
- 2 tbsp hot paprika
- Salt and black pepper to taste
- 1 tbsp cilantro, chopped

Directions:

1. Warm the avocado oil in a pot over medium heat and sear pork for 5 minutes. Put in onion and garlic and cook

for 5 minutes. Stir in stock, paprika, salt, pepper, and buttermilk and bring to a boil; cook for 30 minutes. Top with cilantro.

Nutrition Info:

- Info Per Serving: Calories: 310;Fat: 10g;Protein: 23g;Carbs: 16g.

Savory Tomato Chicken

Servings:4

Cooking Time:90 Minutes

Ingredients:

- 3 tbsp olive oil
- 1 can diced tomatoes,
- 4 chicken breast halves
- 2 whole cloves
- ¼ cup chicken broth
- 2 tbsp tomato paste
- ¼ tsp chili flakes
- 1 tsp ground allspice
- ½ tsp dried mint
- 1 cinnamon stick
- Salt and black pepper to taste

Directions:

1. Place tomatoes, chicken broth, olive oil, tomato paste, chili flakes, mint, allspice, cloves, cinnamon stick, salt, and pepper in a pot over medium heat and bring just to a boil. Then, lower the heat and simmer for 30 minutes. Strain the sauce through a fine-mesh sieve and discard the cloves and cinnamon stick. Let it cool completely.

2. Preheat oven to 350 F. Lay the chicken on a baking dish and pour the sauce over. Bake covered with aluminum foil for 40-45 minutes. Uncover and continue baking for 5 more minutes.

Nutrition Info:

- Info Per Serving: Calories: 259;Fat: 14g;Protein: 24g;Carbs: 11g.

Chicken With Bell Peppers

Servings:4

Cooking Time:65 Minutes

Ingredients:

- 2 tbsp olive oil
- 2 lb chicken breasts, cubed
- 2 garlic cloves, minced
- 1 red onion, chopped
- 2 red bell peppers, chopped
- ¼ tsp cumin, ground

- 2 cups corn
- ½ cup chicken stock
- 1 tsp chili powder

Directions:

1. Warm the olive oil in a skillet over medium heat and sear chicken for 8 minutes on both sides. Put in onion and garlic and cook for another 5 minutes. Stir in bell peppers, cumin, corn, stock, and chili powder. Cook for 45 minutes. Serve.

Nutrition Info:

- Info Per Serving: Calories: 340;Fat: 17g;Protein: 19g;Carbs: 27g.

Slow Cook Lamb Shanks With Cannellini Beans Stew

Servings:12

Cooking Time: 10 Hours 15 Minutes

Ingredients:

- 1 can cannellini beans, rinsed and drained
- 1 large yellow onion, chopped
- 2 medium-sized carrots, diced
- 1 large stalk celery, chopped
- 2 cloves garlic, thinly sliced
- 4 lamb shanks, fat trimmed
- 2 teaspoons tarragon
- ½ teaspoon sea salt
- ¼ teaspoon ground black pepper
- 1 can diced tomatoes, with the juice

Directions:

1. Combine the beans, onion, carrots, celery, and garlic in the slow cooker. Stir to mix well.

2. Add the lamb shanks and sprinkle with tarragon, salt, and ground black pepper.

3. Pour in the tomatoes with juice, then cover the lid and cook on high for an hour.

4. Reduce the heat to low and cook for 9 hours or until the lamb is super tender.

5. Transfer the lamb on a plate, then pour the bean mixture in a colander over a separate bowl to reserve the liquid.

6. Let the liquid sit for 5 minutes until set, then skim the fat from the surface of the liquid. Pour the bean mixture back to the liquid.

7. Remove the bones from the lamb heat and discard the bones. Put the lamb meat and bean mixture back to the slow cooker. Cover and cook to reheat for 15 minutes or until heated through.

8. Pour them on a large serving plate and serve immediately.

Nutrition Info:

- Info Per Serving: Calories: 317;Fat: 9.7g;Protein: 52.1g;Carbs: 7.0g.

Grilled Chicken Breasts With Italian Sauce

Servings:4
Cooking Time:25 Min + Marinating Time

Ingredients:

- ½ cup olive oil
- 2 tbsp rosemary, chopped
- 2 tbsp parsley, chopped
- 1 tsp minced garlic
- 1 lemon, zested and juiced
- Salt and black pepper to taste
- 4 chicken breasts
- 2 tsp basil, chopped

Directions:

1. Combine the olive oil, rosemary, garlic, lemon juice, lemon zest, parsley, salt, and pepper in a plastic bag. Add the chicken and shake to coat. Refrigerate for 2 hours.

2. Heat your grill to medium heat. Remove the chicken breasts from the marinade and grill them for 6-8 minutes per side. Pour the marinade into a saucepan, add 2 tbsp of water and simmer for 2-3 minutes until the sauce thickens. Sprinkle with basil and serve the grilled chicken. Enjoy!

Nutrition Info:

- Info Per Serving: Calories: 449;Fat: 32g;Protein: 38g;Carbs: 2.1g.

Cilantro Turkey Penne With Asparagus

Servings:4
Cooking Time:40 Minutes

Ingredients:

- 3 tbsp olive oil
- 16 oz penne pasta
- 1 lb turkey breast strips
- 1 lb asparagus, chopped
- 1 tsp basil, chopped
- Salt and black pepper to taste
- ½ cup tomato sauce
- 2 tbsp cilantro, chopped

Directions:

1. Bring to a boil salted water in a pot over medium heat and cook penne until "al dente", 8-10 minutes. Drain and set aside; reserve 1 cup of the cooking water.

2. Warm the olive oil in a skillet over medium heat and sear turkey for 4 minutes, stirring periodically. Add in asparagus and sauté for 3-4 more minutes. Pour in the tomato sauce and reserved pasta liquid and bring to a boil; simmer for 20 minutes. Stir in cooked penne, season with salt and pepper, and top with the basil and cilantro to serve.

Nutrition Info:

- Info Per Serving: Calories: 350;Fat: 22g;Protein: 19g;Carbs: 23g.

Greek-style Veggie & Beef In Pita

Servings:2
Cooking Time:30 Minutes

Ingredients:

- Beef
- 1 tbsp olive oil
- ½ medium onion, minced
- 2 garlic cloves, minced
- 6 oz lean ground beef
- 1 tsp dried oregano
- Yogurt Sauce
- ⅓ cup plain Greek yogurt
- 1 oz crumbled feta cheese
- 1 tbsp minced fresh dill
- 1 tbsp minced scallions
- 1 tbsp lemon juice
- Garlic salt to taste
- Sandwiches
- 2 Greek-style pitas, warm
- 6 cherry tomatoes, halved
- 1 cucumber, sliced
- Salt and black pepper to taste

Directions:

1. Warm the 1 tbsp olive oil in a pan over medium heat. Sauté the onion, garlic, and ground for 5-7 minutes, breaking up the meat well. When the meat is no longer pink, drain off any fat and stir in oregano. Turn off the heat.

2. In a small bowl, combine the yogurt, feta, dill, scallions, lemon juice, and garlic salt. Divide the yogurt sauce between the warm pitas. Top with ground beef, cherry tomatoes, and diced cucumber. Season with salt and pepper. Serve.

Nutrition Info:

- Info Per Serving: Calories: 541;Fat: 21g;Protein: 29g;Carbs: 57g.

Chicken Breasts In White Sauce

Servings:4
Cooking Time:30 Minutes
Ingredients:
- 1 cup canned cream of onion soup
- 2 tbsp olive oil
- 1 lb chicken breasts, cubed
- ½ tsp dried basil
- ½ cup flour
- ½ cup white wine
- 1 cup heavy cream
- 4 garlic cloves, minced
- ¼ tsp chili flakes, crushed
- Salt and black pepper to taste
- 2 tbsp parsley, chopped

Directions:
1. In a bowl, combine salt, black pepper, chili flakes, basil, and flour. Add in chicken and toss to coat. Warm the olive oil in a skillet over medium heat. Add in the chicken and cook for 5 minutes, stirring occasionally. Pour in the white wine to scrape any bits from the bottom. Stir in garlic, onion soup, and ½ cup of water. Bring to a boil, then lower the heat, and simmer covered for 15-18 minutes. Stir in heavy cream, top with parsley and chili flakes, and serve.

Nutrition Info:
- Info Per Serving: Calories: 465;Fat: 27g;Protein: 35g;Carbs: 15g.

Coriander Pork Roast

Servings:4
Cooking Time:2 Hours 10 Minutes
Ingredients:
- 2 tbsp olive oil
- 2 lb pork loin roast, boneless
- Salt and black pepper to taste
- 2 garlic cloves, minced
- 1 tsp ground coriander
- 1 tbsp coriander seeds
- 2 tsp red pepper, crushed

Directions:
1. Preheat the oven to 360 F. Toss pork, salt, pepper, garlic, ground coriander, coriander seeds, red pepper, and olive oil in a roasting pan and bake for 2 hours. Serve sliced.

Nutrition Info:

- Info Per Serving: Calories: 310;Fat: 5g;Protein: 16g;Carbs: 7g.

Eggplant & Chicken Skillet

Servings:4
Cooking Time:40 Minutes
Ingredients:
- 2 tbsp olive oil
- 1 lb eggplants, cubed
- Salt and black pepper to taste
- 1 onion, chopped
- 2 garlic cloves, minced
- 1 tsp hot paprika
- 1 tbsp oregano, chopped
- 1 cup chicken stock
- 1 lb chicken breasts, cubed
- 1 cup half and half
- 3 tsp toasted chopped almonds

Directions:
1. Warm the olive oil in a skillet over medium heat and sauté chicken for 8 minutes, stirring often. Mix in eggplants, onion, and garlic and cook for another 5 minutes. Season with salt, pepper, hot paprika, and oregano and pour in the stock. Bring to a boil and simmer for 16 minutes. Stir in half and half for 2 minutes. Serve topped with almonds.

Nutrition Info:
- Info Per Serving: Calories: 400;Fat: 13g;Protein: 26g;Carbs: 22g.

Parsley Eggplant Lamb

Servings:4
Cooking Time:70 Minutes
Ingredients:
- 2 tbsp olive oil
- 1 cup chicken stock
- 1 ½ lb lamb meat, cubed
- 2 eggplants, cubed
- 2 onions, chopped
- 2 tbsp tomato paste
- 2 tbsp parsley, chopped
- 4 garlic cloves, minced

Directions:
1. Warm the olive oil in a skillet over medium heat and cook onions and garlic for 4 minutes. Put in lamb and cook for 6 minutes. Stir in eggplants and tomato paste for 5 minutes. Pour in the stock and bring to a boil. Cook for

another 50 minutes, stirring often. Serve garnished with parsley.

Nutrition Info:

- Info Per Serving: Calories: 310;Fat: 19g;Protein: 15g;Carbs: 23g.

Traditional Meatball Soup

Servings:6

Cooking Time:35 Minutes

Ingredients:

- 2 tbsp olive oil
- 1 can diced tomatoes
- ½ cup rice, rinsed
- 12 oz ground beef
- 2 shallots, chopped
- 1 tbsp dried thyme
- 1 carrot, chopped
- 1 tsp garlic powder
- 5 garlic cloves, minced
- 6 cups chicken broth
- ¼ cup chopped basil leaves
- Salt and black pepper to taste

Directions:

1. Combine ground beef, shallots, garlic powder, thyme, salt, and pepper in a bowl. Make balls out of the mixture and reserve. Warm the olive oil in a pot over medium heat and sauté the garlic and carrot for 2 minutes. Mix in meatballs, rice, tomatoes, broth, salt, and pepper and bring to a boil. Lower the heat and simmer for 18 minutes. Top with basil.

Nutrition Info:

- Info Per Serving: Calories: 265;Fat: 9.8g;Protein: 24g;Carbs: 19g.

Drunken Lamb Bake

Servings:4

Cooking Time:90 Minutes

Ingredients:

- 3 tbsp butter
- 2 lb leg of lamb, sliced
- 3 garlic cloves, chopped
- 2 onions, chopped
- 3 cups vegetable stock
- 2 cups dry red wine
- 2 tbsp tomato pastes
- 1 tsp thyme, chopped
- Salt and black pepper to taste

Directions:

1. Preheat the oven to 360 F. Melt butter in a skillet over medium heat. Sear lamb for 10 minutes on both sides. Remove to a roasting pan. In the same skillet, add and cook onions and garlic for 5 minutes. Stir in stock, red wine, tomato paste, thyme, salt, and pepper and bring to a boil. Cook for 10 minutes and pour over lamb. Bake for 1 hour.

Nutrition Info:

- Info Per Serving: Calories: 290;Fat: 22g;Protein: 19g;Carbs: 17g.

Fennel Beef Ribs

Servings:4

Cooking Time:2 Hours 10 Minutes

Ingredients:

- 2 tbsp olive oil
- 2 lb beef ribs
- 2 garlic cloves, minced
- 1 onion, chopped
- ½ cup chicken stock
- 1 tbsp ground fennel seeds

Directions:

1. Preheat oven to 360 F. Mix garlic, onion, stock, olive oil, fennel seeds, and beef ribs in a roasting pan and bake for 2 hours. Serve hot with salad.

Nutrition Info:

- Info Per Serving: Calories: 300;Fat: 10g;Protein: 25g;Carbs: 18g.

Slow Cooker Brussel Sprout & Chicken

Servings:4

Cooking Time:8 Hours 20 Minutes

Ingredients:

- 2 tbsp olive oil
- 1 lb Brussels sprouts, halved
- 2 lb chicken breasts, cubed
- 1 ½ cups veggie stock
- 2 red onions, sliced
- 2 garlic cloves, minced
- 1 tbsp sweet paprika
- ½ cup tomato sauce
- Salt and black pepper to taste

Directions:

1. Warm the olive oil in a skillet over medium heat and sear the chicken for 10 minutes on all sides. Remove to your slow cooker. Add in onions, stock, garlic, paprika,

Brussels sprouts, tomato sauce, salt, pepper, and dill. Cover the lid and cook for 8 hours on Low. Serve immediately.

Nutrition Info:

- Info Per Serving: Calories: 302;Fat: 15g;Protein: 16g;Carbs: 17g.

Beef Filet Mignon In Mushroom Sauce

Servings:2

Cooking Time:25 Minutes

Ingredients:

- 8 oz cremini mushrooms, quartered
- 2 tbsp olive oil
- 2 filet mignon steaks
- 1 shallot, minced
- 2 tsp flour
- 2 tsp tomato paste
- ½ cup red wine
- 1 cup chicken stock
- ½ tsp dried thyme
- 1 fresh rosemary sprig
- 1 tsp herbes de Provence
- Salt and black pepper to taste
- ¼ tsp garlic powder
- ¼ tsp shallot powder
- ¼ tsp mustard powder

Directions:

1. Warm 1 tablespoon of olive oil in a saucepan over medium heat. Add the mushrooms and shallot and stir-fry for 5-8 minutes. Stir in the flour and tomato paste and cook for another 30 seconds. Pour in the wine and scrape up any browned bits from the sauté pan. Add the chicken stock, thyme, and rosemary. Bring it to a boil and cook until the sauce thickens, 2-4 minutes. In a small bowl, mix the herbes de Provence, salt, garlic powder, shallot powder, mustard powder, salt, and pepper. Rub the beef with the herb mixture on both sides. Warm the remaining olive oil in a sauté over medium heat. Sear the beef for 2-3 minutes on each side. Serve topped with mushroom sauce.

Nutrition Info:

- Info Per Serving: Calories: 385;Fat: 20g;Protein: 25g;Carbs: 15g.

Sausage & Herb Eggs

Servings:2

Cooking Time:20 Minutes

Ingredients:

- 2 tbsp olive oil
- ½ cup leeks, chopped
- ½ lb pork sausage, crumbled
- 4 eggs, whisked
- 1 thyme sprig, chopped
- 1 tsp habanero pepper, minced
- ½ tsp dried marjoram
- 1 tsp garlic puree
- ½ cup green olives, sliced
- Salt and black pepper to taste

Directions:

1. Warm the olive oil in a skillet over medium heat. Sauté the leeks until they are just tender, about 4 minutes. Add the garlic, habanero pepper, salt, black pepper, and sausage; cook for 8 minutes, stirring frequently. Pour in the eggs and sprinkle with thyme and marjoram. Cook for an additional 4 minutes, stirring with a spoon. Garnish with olives. Serve.

Nutrition Info:

- Info Per Serving: Calories: 460;Fat: 41g;Protein: 16g;Carbs: 6g.

Fish And Seafood Recipes

Instant Pot Poached Salmon

Servings:4

Cooking Time: 3 Minutes

Ingredients:

- 1 lemon, sliced ¼ inch thick
- 4 skinless salmon fillets, 1½ inches thick
- ½ teaspoon salt
- ¼ teaspoon pepper
- ½ cup water

Directions:

1. Layer the lemon slices in the bottom of the Instant Pot.

2. Season the salmon with salt and pepper, then arrange the salmon (skin- side down) on top of the lemon slices. Pour in the water.

3. Secure the lid. Select the Manual mode and set the cooking time for 3 minutes at High Pressure.

4. Once cooking is complete, do a quick pressure release. Carefully open the lid.

5. Serve warm.

Nutrition Info:

- Info Per Serving: Calories: 350;Fat: 23.0g;Protein: 35.0g;Carbs: 0g.

Slow Cooker Salmon In Foil

Servings:2

Cooking Time: 2 Hours

Ingredients:

- 2 salmon fillets
- 1 tablespoon olive oil
- 2 cloves garlic, minced
- ½ tablespoon lime juice
- 1 teaspoon finely chopped fresh parsley
- ¼ teaspoon black pepper

Directions:

1. Spread a length of foil onto a work surface and place the salmon fillets in the middle.

2. Mix together the olive oil, garlic, lime juice, parsley, and black pepper in a small bowl. Brush the mixture over the fillets. Fold the foil over and crimp the sides to make a packet.

3. Place the packet into the slow cooker, cover, and cook on High for 2 hours, or until the fish flakes easily with a fork.

4. Serve hot.

Nutrition Info:

- Info Per Serving: Calories: 446;Fat: 20.7g;Protein: 65.4g;Carbs: 1.5g.

Pesto Shrimp Over Zoodles

Servings:4

Cooking Time: 10 Minutes

Ingredients:

- 1 pound fresh shrimp, peeled and deveined
- Salt and freshly ground black pepper, to taste
- 2 tablespoons extra-virgin olive oil
- ½ small onion, slivered
- 8 ounces store-bought jarred pesto
- ¾ cup crumbled goat or feta cheese, plus additional for serving
- 2 large zucchini, spiralized, for serving
- ¼ cup chopped flat-leaf Italian parsley, for garnish

Directions:

1. In a bowl, season the shrimp with salt and pepper. Set aside.

2. In a large skillet, heat the olive oil over medium-high heat. Sauté the onion until just golden, 5 to 6 minutes.

3. Reduce the heat to low and add the pesto and cheese, whisking to combine and melt the cheese. Bring to a low simmer and add the shrimp. Reduce the heat back to low and cover. Cook until the shrimp is cooked through and pink, about 3 to 4 minutes.

4. Serve the shrimp warm over zoodles, garnishing with chopped parsley and additional crumbled cheese.

Nutrition Info:

- Info Per Serving: Calories: 491;Fat: 35.0g;Protein: 29.0g;Carbs: 15.0g.

Crispy Sole Fillets

Servings:4

Cooking Time:10 Minutes

Ingredients:

- ¼ cup olive oil
- ½ cup flour
- ½ tsp paprika
- 8 skinless sole fillets
- Salt and black pepper to taste
- 4 lemon wedges

Directions:

1. Warm the olive oil in a skillet over medium heat. Mix the flour with paprika in a shallow dish. Coat the fish with the flour, shaking off any excess. Sear the sole fillets for 2-3 minutes per side until lightly browned. Serve with lemon wedges.

Nutrition Info:

- Info Per Serving: Calories: 219;Fat: 15g;Protein: 8.7g;Carbs: 13g.

Date & Hazelnut Crusted Barramundi

Servings:2

Cooking Time:25 Minutes

Ingredients:

- 2 tbsp olive oil
- 2 barramundi fillets, boneless
- 1 shallot, sliced
- 4 lemon slices
- ½ lemon, zested and juiced
- 1 cup baby spinach
- ¼ cup hazelnuts, chopped
- 4 dates, pitted and chopped
- Salt and black pepper to taste

Directions:

1. Preheat oven to 380 F. Sprinkle barramundi with salt and pepper and place on 2 parchment paper pieces. Top each fillet with lemon slices, lemon juice, shallot, lemon zest, spinach, hazelnuts, dates, and parsley. Sprinkle each fillet with 1 tbsp of oil and fold the paper around it. Place them on a baking sheet and bake for 12 minutes. Serve and enjoy!

Nutrition Info:

- Info Per Serving: Calories: 240;Fat: 17g;Protein: 7g;Carbs: 26g.

Baked Lemon Salmon

Servings:4

Cooking Time: 20 Minutes

Ingredients:

- ¼ teaspoon dried thyme
- Zest and juice of ½ lemon
- ¼ teaspoon salt
- ½ teaspoon freshly ground black pepper
- 1 pound salmon fillet
- Nonstick cooking spray

Directions:

1. Preheat the oven to 425ºF. Coat a baking sheet with nonstick cooking spray.

2. Mix together the thyme, lemon zest and juice, salt, and pepper in a small bowl and stir to incorporate.

3. Arrange the salmon, skin-side down, on the coated baking sheet. Spoon the thyme mixture over the salmon and spread it all over.

4. Bake in the preheated oven for about 15 to 20 minutes, or until the fish flakes apart easily. Serve warm.

Nutrition Info:

- Info Per Serving: Calories: 162;Fat: 7.0g;Protein: 23.1g;Carbs: 1.0g.

Seared Salmon With Lemon Cream Sauce

Servings:4

Cooking Time: 20 Minutes

Ingredients:

- 4 salmon fillets
- Sea salt and freshly ground black pepper, to taste
- 1 tablespoon extra-virgin olive oil
- ½ cup low-sodium vegetable broth
- Juice and zest of 1 lemon
- 1 teaspoon chopped fresh thyme
- ½ cup fat-free sour cream
- 1 teaspoon honey
- 1 tablespoon chopped fresh chives

Directions:

1. Preheat the oven to 400ºF.

2. Season the salmon lightly on both sides with salt and pepper.

3. Place a large ovenproof skillet over medium-high heat and add the olive oil.

4. Sear the salmon fillets on both sides until golden, about 3 minutes per side.

5. Transfer the salmon to a baking dish and bake in the preheated oven until just cooked through, about 10 minutes.

6. Meanwhile, whisk together the vegetable broth, lemon juice and zest, and thyme in a small saucepan over medium-high heat until the liquid reduces by about one-quarter, about 5 minutes.

7. Whisk in the sour cream and honey.

8. Stir in the chives and serve the sauce over the salmon.

Nutrition Info:

- Info Per Serving: Calories: 310;Fat: 18.0g;Protein 29.0g;Carbs: 6.0g.

Vegetable & Shrimp Roast

Servings:4

Cooking Time:30 Minutes

Ingredients:

- 2 lb shrimp, peeled and deveined
- 4 tbsp olive oil
- 2 bell peppers, cut into chunks
- 2 fennel bulbs, cut into wedges
- 2 red onions, cut into wedges
- 4 garlic cloves, unpeeled
- 8 Kalamata olives, halved
- 1 tsp lemon zest, grated
- 2 tsp oregano, dried
- 2 tbsp parsley, chopped
- Salt and black pepper to taste

Directions:

1. Preheat the oven to 390 F. Place bell peppers, garlic, fennel, red onions, and olives in a roasting tray. Add in the lemon zest, oregano, half of the olive oil, salt, and pepper and toss to coat; roast for 15 minutes. Coat the shrimp with the remaining olive oil and pour over the veggies; roast for another 7 minutes. Serve topped with parsley.

Nutrition Info:

- Info Per Serving: Calories: 350;Fat: 20g;Protein: 1g;Carbs: 35g.

Veggie & Clam Stew With Chickpeas

Servings:4

Cooking Time:40 Minutes

Ingredients:

- 2 tbsp olive oil
- 1 yellow onion, chopped
- 1 fennel bulb, chopped
- 1 carrot, chopped
- 1 red bell pepper, chopped
- 2 garlic cloves, minced
- 3 tbsp tomato paste
- 16 oz canned chickpeas, drained
- 1 tsp dried thyme
- ¼ tsp smoked paprika
- Salt and black pepper to taste
- 1 lb clams, scrubbed

Directions:

1. Warm olive oil in a pot over medium heat and sauté fennel, onion, bell pepper, and carrot for 5 minutes until they're tender. Stir in garlic and tomato paste and cook for

another minute. Mix in the chickpeas, thyme, paprika, salt, pepper, and 2 cups of water and bring to a boil; cook for 20 minutes.

2. Rinse the clams under cold, running water. Discard any clams that remain open when tapped with your fingers. Put the unopened clams into the pot and cook everything for 4-5 minutes until the shells have opened. When finished, discard any clams that haven't opened fully during the cooking process. Adjust the seasoning with salt and pepper. Serve.

Nutrition Info:

- Info Per Serving: Calories: 460;Fat: 13g;Protein: 35g;Carbs: 48g.

Herby Cod Skewers

Servings:4

Cooking Time:30 Minutes

Ingredients:

- 1 lb cod fillets, cut into chunks
- 2 sweet peppers, cut into chunks
- 2 tbsp olive oil
- 2 oranges, juiced
- 1 tbsp Dijon mustard
- 1 tsp dried dill
- 1 tsp dried parsley
- Salt and black pepper to taste

Directions:

1. Mix olive oil, orange juice, dill, parsley, mustard, salt, and pepper in a bowl. Stir in cod to coat. Allow sitting for 10 minutes. Heat the grill over medium heat. Thread the cod and peppers onto skewers. Grill for 7-8 minutes, turning regularly until the fish is cooked through.

Nutrition Info:

- Info Per Serving: Calories: 244;Fat: 8g;Protein: 27g;Carbs: 15.5g.

Moules Mariniere (mussels In Wine Sauce)

Servings:4

Cooking Time:15 Minutes

Ingredients:

- 4 tbsp butter
- 4 lb cleaned mussels
- 2 cups dry white wine
- ½ tsp sea salt
- 6 garlic cloves, minced
- 1 shallot, diced

- ½ cup chopped parsley
- Juice of ½ lemon

Directions:

1. Pour the white wine, salt, garlic, shallots, and ¼ cup of the parsley into a large saucepan over medium heat. Cover and bring to boil. Add the mussels and simmer just until all of the mussels open, about 6 minutes. Do not overcook. With a slotted spoon, remove the mussels to a bowl. Add the butter and lemon juice to the saucepan, stir, and pour the broth over the mussels. Garnish with the remaining parsley and serve with a crusty, wholegrain baguette.

Nutrition Info:

- Info Per Serving: Calories: 528;Fat: 24g;Protein: 55g;Carbs: 20g.

Herby Tuna Gratin

Servings:4
Cooking Time:20 Minutes

Ingredients:

- 10 oz canned tuna, flaked
- 4 eggs, whisked
- ½ cup mozzarella, shredded
- 1 tbsp chives, chopped
- 1 tbsp parsley, chopped
- Salt and black pepper to taste

Directions:

1. Preheat the oven to 360 F. Mix tuna, eggs, chives, parsley, salt, and pepper in a bowl. Transfer to a greased baking dish and bake for 15 minutes. Scatter cheese on top and let sit for 5 minutes. Cut before serving.

Nutrition Info:

- Info Per Serving: Calories: 300;Fat: 15g;Protein: 7g;Carbs: 13g.

Hake Fillet In Herby Tomato Sauce

Servings:4
Cooking Time:30 Minutes

Ingredients:

- 2 tbsp olive oil
- 1 onion, sliced thin
- 1 fennel bulb, sliced
- Salt and black pepper to taste
- 4 garlic cloves, minced
- 1 tsp fresh thyme, chopped
- 1 can diced tomatoes,
- ½ cup dry white wine
- 4 skinless hake fillets

- 2 tbsp fresh basil, chopped

Directions:

1. Warm the olive oil in a skillet over medium heat. Sauté the onion and fennel for about 5 minutes until softened. Stir in garlic and thyme and cook for about 30 seconds until fragrant. Pour in tomatoes and wine and bring to simmer.

2. Season the hake with salt and pepper. Nestle hake skinned side down into the tomato sauce and spoon some sauce over the top. Bring to simmer. Cook for 10-12 minutes until hake easily flakes with a fork. Sprinkle with basil and serve.

Nutrition Info:

- Info Per Serving: Calories: 452;Fat: 9.9g;Protein: 78g;Carbs: 9.7g.

Baked Halibut Steaks With Vegetables

Servings:4
Cooking Time: 20 Minutes

Ingredients:

- 2 teaspoon olive oil, divided
- 1 clove garlic, peeled and minced
- ½ cup minced onion
- 1 cup diced zucchini
- 2 cups diced fresh tomatoes
- 2 tablespoons chopped fresh basil
- ¼ teaspoon salt
- ¼ teaspoon ground black pepper
- 4 halibut steaks
- ⅓ cup crumbled feta cheese

Directions:

1. Preheat oven to 450ºF. Coat a shallow baking dish lightly with 1 teaspoon of olive oil.

2. In a medium saucepan, heat the remaining 1 teaspoon of olive oil.

3. Add the garlic, onion, and zucchini and mix well. Cook for 5 minutes, stirring occasionally, or until the zucchini is softened.

4. Remove the saucepan from the heat and stir in the tomatoes, basil, salt, and pepper.

5. Place the halibut steaks in the coated baking dish in a single layer. Spread the zucchini mixture evenly over the steaks. Scatter the top with feta cheese.

6. Bake in the preheated oven for about 15 minutes, or until the fish flakes when pressed lightly with a fork. Serve hot.

Nutrition Info:

- Info Per Serving: Calories: 258;Fat: 7.6g;Protein 38.6g;Carbs: 6.5g.

Spiced Citrus Sole

Servings:4
Cooking Time: 10 Minutes
Ingredients:

- 1 teaspoon garlic powder
- 1 teaspoon chili powder
- ½ teaspoon lemon zest
- ½ teaspoon lime zest
- ¼ teaspoon smoked paprika
- ¼ teaspoon freshly ground black pepper
- Pinch sea salt
- 4 sole fillets, patted dry
- 1 tablespoon extra-virgin olive oil
- 2 teaspoons freshly squeezed lime juice

Directions:

1. Preheat the oven to 450ºF. Line a baking sheet with aluminum foil and set aside.
2. Mix together the garlic powder, chili powder, lemon zest, lime zest, paprika, pepper, and salt in a small bowl until well combined.
3. Arrange the sole fillets on the prepared baking sheet and rub the spice mixture all over the fillets until well coated. Drizzle the olive oil and lime juice over the fillets.
4. Bake in the preheated oven for about 8 minutes until flaky.
5. Remove from the heat to a plate and serve.

Nutrition Info:

- Info Per Serving: Calories: 183;Fat: 5.0g;Protein: 32.1g;Carbs: 0g.

Oil–poached Cod

Servings:4
Cooking Time:20 Minutes
Ingredients:

- 4 cod fillets, skins removed
- 3 cups olive oil
- Salt and black pepper to taste
- 1 lemon, zested and juiced
- 3 fresh thyme sprigs

Directions:

1. Heat the olive oil with thyme sprigs in a pot over low heat. Gently add the cod fillets and poach them for about 6 minutes or until the fish is completely opaque. Using a slotted spoon, carefully remove the fish to a plate lined with paper towels. Sprinkle with lemon zest, salt, and pepper. Drizzle with lemon juice and serve immediately.

Nutrition Info:

- Info Per Serving: Calories: 292;Fat: 34g;Protein: 18g;Carbs: 1g.

Garlic Shrimp With Arugula Pesto

Servings:2
Cooking Time: 5 Minutes
Ingredients:

- 3 cups lightly packed arugula
- ½ cup lightly packed basil leaves
- ¼ cup walnuts
- 3 tablespoons olive oil
- 3 medium garlic cloves
- 2 tablespoons grated Parmesan cheese
- 1 tablespoon freshly squeezed lemon juice
- Salt and freshly ground black pepper, to taste
- 1 package zucchini noodles
- 8 ounces cooked, shelled shrimp
- 2 Roma tomatoes, diced

Directions:

1. Process the arugula, basil, walnuts, olive oil, garlic, Parmesan cheese, and lemon juice in a food processor until smooth, scraping down the sides as needed. Season with salt and pepper to taste.
2. Heat a skillet over medium heat. Add the pesto, zucchini noodles, and cooked shrimp. Toss to combine the sauce over the noodles and shrimp, and cook until heated through.
3. Taste and season with more salt and pepper as needed. Serve topped with the diced tomatoes.

Nutrition Info:

- Info Per Serving: Calories: 435;Fat: 30.2g;Protein: 33.0g;Carbs: 15.1g.

Shrimp And Pea Paella

Servings:2
Cooking Time: 60 Minutes
Ingredients:

- 2 tablespoons olive oil
- 1 garlic clove, minced
- ½ large onion, minced
- 1 cup diced tomato
- ½ cup short-grain rice
- ½ teaspoon sweet paprika
- ½ cup dry white wine
- 1¼ cups low-sodium chicken stock
- 8 ounces large raw shrimp
- 1 cup frozen peas

- ¼ cup jarred roasted red peppers, cut into strips
- Salt, to taste

Directions:

1. Heat the olive oil in a large skillet over medium-high heat.

2. Add the garlic and onion and sauté for 3 minutes, or until the onion is softened.

3. Add the tomato, rice, and paprika and stir for 3 minutes to toast the rice.

4. Add the wine and chicken stock and stir to combine. Bring the mixture to a boil.

5. Cover and reduce the heat to medium-low, and simmer for 45 minutes, or until the rice is just about tender and most of the liquid has been absorbed.

6. Add the shrimp, peas, and roasted red peppers. Cover and cook for an additional 5 minutes. Season with salt to taste and serve.

Nutrition Info:

- Info Per Serving: Calories: 646;Fat: 27.1g;Protein: 42.0g;Carbs: 59.7g.

Salmon Packets

Servings:4
Cooking Time:25 Minutes

Ingredients:

- 2 tbsp olive oil
- ½ cup apple juice
- 4 salmon fillets
- 4 tsp lemon zest
- 4 tbsp chopped parsley
- Salt and black pepper to taste

Directions:

1. Preheat oven to 380F. Brush salmon with olive oil and season with salt and pepper. Cut four pieces of nonstick baking paper and divide the salmon between them. Top each one with apple juice, lemon zest, and parsley.

2. Wrap the paper to make packets and arrange them on a baking sheet. Cook for 15 minutes until the salmon is cooked through. Remove the packets to a serving plate, open them, and drizzle with cooking juices to serve.

Nutrition Info:

- Info Per Serving: Calories: 495;Fat: 21g;Protein: 55g;Carbs: 5g.

Lemon Cioppino

Servings:6
Cooking Time:6 Minutes

Ingredients:

- 1 lb mussels, scrubbed, debearded
- 1 lb large shrimp, peeled and deveined
- 1 ½ lb haddock fillets, cut into chunks
- 3 tbsp olive oil
- 1 fennel bulb, thinly sliced
- 1 onion, chopped
- 3 large shallots, chopped
- Salt to taste
- 4 garlic cloves, minced
- ¼ tsp red pepper flakes
- ¼ cup tomato paste
- 1 can diced tomatoes
- 1 ½ cups dry white wine
- 5 cups vegetable stock
- 1 bay leaf
- 1 lb clams, scrubbed
- 2 tbsp basil, chopped

Directions:

1. Warm the olive oil in a large pot over medium heat. Sauté the fennel, onion, garlic, and shallots for 8-10 minutes until tender. Add the red pepper flakes and sauté for 2 minutes. Stir in the tomato paste, tomatoes with their juices, wine, stock, salt, and bay leaf. Cover and bring to a simmer. Lower the heat to low and simmer for 30 minutes until the flavors blend.

2. Pour in the clams and mussels and cook for about 5 minutes. Add the shrimp and fish. Simmer gently until the fish and shrimp are just cooked through, 5 minutes. Discard any clams and mussels that refuse to open and bay leaf. Top with basil.

Nutrition Info:

- Info Per Serving: Calories: 163;Fat: 4.1g;Protein: 22g;Carbs: 8.3g.

Canned Sardine Donburi (rice Bowl)

Servings:4
Cooking Time: 40 To 50 Minutes

Ingredients:

- 4 cups water
- 2 cups brown rice, rinsed well
- ½ teaspoon salt
- 3 cans sardines packed in water, drained

- 3 scallions, sliced thin
- 1-inch piece fresh ginger, grated
- 4 tablespoons sesame oil

Directions:

1. Place the water, brown rice, and salt to a large saucepan and stir to combine. Allow the mixture to boil over high heat.

2. Once boiling, reduce the heat to low, and cook covered for 45 to 50 minutes, or until the rice is tender.

3. Meanwhile, roughly mash the sardines with a fork in a medium bowl.

4. When the rice is done, stir in the mashed sardines, scallions, and ginger.

5. Divide the mixture into four bowls. Top each bowl with a drizzle of sesame oil. Serve warm.

Nutrition Info:

- Info Per Serving: Calories: 603;Fat: 23.6g;Protein: 25.2g;Carbs: 73.8g.

10-minute Cod With Parsley Pistou

Servings:4

Cooking Time: 10 Minutes

Ingredients:

- 1 cup packed roughly chopped fresh flat-leaf Italian parsley
- Zest and juice of 1 lemon
- 1 to 2 small garlic cloves, minced
- 1 teaspoon salt
- ½ teaspoon freshly ground black pepper
- 1 cup extra-virgin olive oil, divided
- 1 pound cod fillets, cut into 4 equal-sized pieces

Directions:

1. Make the pistou: Place the parsley, lemon zest and juice, garlic, salt, and pepper in a food processor until finely chopped.

2. With the food processor running, slowly drizzle in ¾ cup of olive oil until a thick sauce forms. Set aside.

3. Heat the remaining ¼ cup of olive oil in a large skillet over medium-high heat.

4. Add the cod fillets, cover, and cook each side for 4 to 5 minutes, until browned and cooked through.

5. Remove the cod fillets from the heat to a plate and top each with generous spoonfuls of the prepared pistou. Serve immediately.

Nutrition Info:

- Info Per Serving: Calories: 580;Fat: 54.6g;Protein: 21.1g;Carbs: 2.8g.

Dill Smoked Salmon & Eggplant Rolls

Servings:4

Cooking Time:20 Minutes

Ingredients:

- 2 eggplants, lengthwise cut into thin slices
- 2 tbsp olive oil
- 1 cup ricotta cheese, soft
- 4 oz smoked salmon, chopped
- 2 tsp lemon zest, grated
- 1 small red onion, sliced
- Salt and pepper to the taste

Directions:

1. Mix salmon, cheese, lemon zest, onion, salt, and pepper in a bowl. Grease the eggplant with olive oil and grill them on a preheated grill pan for 3-4 minutes per side. Set aside to cool. Spread the cooled eggplant slices with the salmon mixture. Roll out and secure with toothpicks and serve.

Nutrition Info:

- Info Per Serving: Calories: 310;Fat: 25g;Protein: 12g;Carbs: 16g.

Farro & Trout Bowls With Avocado

Servings:4

Cooking Time:50 Minutes

Ingredients:

- 4 tbsp olive oil
- 8 trout fillets, boneless
- 1 cup farro
- Juice of 2 lemons
- Salt and black pepper to taste
- 1 avocado, chopped
- ¼ cup balsamic vinegar
- 1 garlic cloves, minced
- ¼ cup parsley, chopped
- ¼ cup mint, chopped
- 2 tbsp yellow mustard

Directions:

1. Boil salted water in a pot over medium heat and stir in farro. Simmer for 30 minutes and drain. Remove to a bowl and combine with lemon juice, mustard, garlic, salt, pepper, and half olive oil. Set aside. Mash the avocado with a fork in a bowl and mix with vinegar, salt, pepper, parsley, and mint.

2. Warm the remaining oil in a skillet over medium heat and brown trout fillets skin-side down for 10 minutes on both sides. Let cool and cut into pieces. Put over farro and stir in avocado dressing. Serve immediately.

* Info Per Serving: Calories: 290;Fat: 13g;Protein: 37g;Carbs: 6g.

Lemony Sea Bass

Servings:4

Cooking Time:25 Minutes

Ingredients:

* 1 tbsp butter, melted
* 4 skinless sea bass fillets
* Salt and black pepper to taste
* ½ tsp onion powder

Directions:

1. Preheat oven to 425 F. Rub the fish with salt, pepper, and onion powder and place on a greased baking dish. Drizzle the butter all over and bake for 20 minutes or until opaque.

Nutrition Info:

* Info Per Serving: Calories: 159;Fat: 6g;Protein: 23.8g;Carbs: 1.2g.

Lemon Shrimp With Black Olives

Servings:4

Cooking Time:25 Minutes

Ingredients:

* 1 lb shrimp, peeled and deveined
* 3 tbsp olive oil
* 1 lemon, juiced
* 1 tbsp flour
* 1 cup fish stock
* Salt and black pepper to taste
* 1 cup black olives, halved
* 1 tbsp rosemary, chopped

Directions:

1. Warm the olive oil in a skillet over medium heat and sear shrimp for 4 minutes on both sides; set aside. In the same skillet over low heat, stir in the flour for 2-3 minutes.

2. Gradually pour in the fish stock and lemon juice while stirring and simmer for 3-4 minutes until the sauce thickens. Adjust the seasoning with salt and pepper and mix in shrimp, olives, and rosemary. Serve immediately.

Nutrition Info:

* Info Per Serving: Calories: 240;Fat: 16g;Protein: 9g;Carbs: 16g.

Easy Breaded Shrimp

Servings:4

Cooking Time: 4 To 6 Minutes

Ingredients:

* 2 large eggs
* 1 tablespoon water
* 2 cups seasoned Italian bread crumbs
* 1 teaspoon salt
* 1 cup flour
* 1 pound large shrimp, peeled and deveined
* Extra-virgin olive oil, as needed

Directions:

1. In a small bowl, beat the eggs with the water, then transfer to a shallow dish.

2. Add the bread crumbs and salt to a separate shallow dish, then mix well.

3. Place the flour into a third shallow dish.

4. Coat the shrimp in the flour, then the beaten egg, and finally the bread crumbs. Place on a plate and repeat with all of the shrimp.

5. Heat a skillet over high heat. Pour in enough olive oil to coat the bottom of the skillet. Cook the shrimp in the hot skillet for 2 to 3 minutes on each side. Remove and drain on a paper towel. Serve warm.

Nutrition Info:

* Info Per Serving: Calories: 714;Fat: 34.0g;Protein: 37.0g;Carbs: 63.0g.

Hazelnut Crusted Sea Bass

Servings:2

Cooking Time: 15 Minutes

Ingredients:

* 2 tablespoons almond butter
* 2 sea bass fillets
* ⅓ cup roasted hazelnuts
* A pinch of cayenne pepper

Directions:

1. Preheat the oven to 425ºF. Line a baking dish with waxed paper.

2. Brush the almond butter over the fillets.

3. Pulse the hazelnuts and cayenne in a food processor. Coat the sea bass with the hazelnut mixture, then transfer to the baking dish.

4. Bake in the preheated oven for about 15 minutes. Cool for 5 minutes before serving.

Nutrition Info:

• Info Per Serving: Calories: 468;Fat: 30.8g;Protein: 40.0g;Carbs: 8.8g.

Garlic Skillet Salmon

Servings:4

Cooking Time: 14 To 16 Minutes

Ingredients:

- 1 tablespoon extra-virgin olive oil
- 2 garlic cloves, minced
- 1 teaspoon smoked paprika
- 1½ cups grape or cherry tomatoes, quartered
- 1 jar roasted red peppers, drained and chopped
- 1 tablespoon water
- ¼ teaspoon freshly ground black pepper
- ¼ teaspoon kosher or sea salt
- 1 pound salmon fillets, skin removed and cut into 8 pieces
- 1 tablespoon freshly squeezed lemon juice

Directions:

1. In a large skillet over medium heat, heat the oil. Add the garlic and smoked paprika and cook for 1 minute, stirring often. Add the tomatoes, roasted peppers, water, black pepper, and salt. Turn up the heat to medium-high, bring to a simmer, and cook for 3 minutes, stirring occasionally and smashing the tomatoes with a wooden spoon toward the end of the cooking time.

2. Add the salmon to the skillet, and spoon some of the sauce over the top. Cover and cook for 10 to 12 minutes, or until the salmon is cooked through and just starts to flake.

3. Remove the skillet from the heat, and drizzle lemon juice over the top of the fish. Stir the sauce, then break up the salmon into chunks with a fork. Serve hot.

Nutrition Info:

- Info Per Serving: Calories: 255;Fat: 11.7g;Protein: 24.2g;Carbs: 5.9g.

Shrimp Quinoa Bowl With Black Olives

Servings:4

Cooking Time:20 Minutes

Ingredients:

- 10 black olives, pitted and halved
- ¼ cup olive oil
- 1 cup quinoa
- 1 lemon, cut in wedges
- 1 lb shrimp, peeled and cooked
- 2 tomatoes, sliced
- 2 bell peppers, thinly sliced
- 1 red onion, chopped
- 1 tsp dried dill
- 1 tbsp fresh parsley, chopped
- Salt and black pepper to taste

Directions:

1. Place the quinoa in a pot and cover with 2 cups of water over medium heat. Bring to a boil, reduce the heat, and simmer for 12-15 minutes or until tender. Remove from heat and fluff it with a fork. Mix in the quinoa with olive oil, dill, parsley, salt, and black pepper. Stir in tomatoes, bell peppers, olives, and onion. Serve decorated with shrimp and lemon wedges.

Nutrition Info:

- Info Per Serving: Calories: 662;Fat: 21g;Protein: 79g;Carbs: 38g.

Vegetable Mains And Meatless Recipes

Roasted Celery Root With Yogurt Sauce

Servings:6
Cooking Time:50 Minutes
Ingredients:

- 3 tbsp olive oil
- 3 celery roots, sliced
- Salt and black pepper to taste
- ¼ cup plain yogurt
- ¼ tsp grated lemon zest
- 1 tsp lemon juice
- 1 tsp sesame seeds, toasted
- 1 tsp coriander seeds, crushed
- ¼ tsp dried thyme
- ¼ tsp chili powder
- ¼ cup fresh cilantro, chopped

Directions:

1. Preheat oven to 425 F. Place the celery slices on a baking sheet. Sprinkle them with olive oil, salt, and pepper. Roast for 25-30 minutes. Flip each piece and continue to roast for 10-15 minutes until celery root is very tender and sides touching sheet are browned. Transfer celery to a serving platter.
2. Whisk yogurt, lemon zest and juice, and salt together in a bowl. In a separate bowl, combine sesame seeds, coriander seeds, thyme, chili powder, and salt. Drizzle celery root with yogurt sauce and sprinkle with seed mixture and cilantro.

Nutrition Info:

- Info Per Serving: Calories: 75;Fat: 7.5g;Protein: 0.7g;Carbs: 1.8g.

Veggie-stuffed Portabello Mushrooms

Servings:6
Cooking Time: 24 To 25 Minutes
Ingredients:

- 3 tablespoons extra-virgin olive oil, divided
- 1 cup diced onion
- 2 garlic cloves, minced
- 1 large zucchini, diced
- 3 cups chopped mushrooms
- 1 cup chopped tomato
- 1 teaspoon dried oregano
- ¼ teaspoon kosher salt
- ¼ teaspoon crushed red pepper
- 6 large portabello mushrooms, stems and gills removed
- Cooking spray
- 4 ounces fresh Mozzarella cheese, shredded

Directions:

1. In a large skillet over medium heat, heat 2 tablespoons of the oil. Add the onion and sauté for 4 minutes. Stir in the garlic and sauté for 1 minute.
2. Stir in the zucchini, mushrooms, tomato, oregano, salt and red pepper. Cook for 10 minutes, stirring constantly. Remove from the heat.
3. Meanwhile, heat a grill pan over medium-high heat.
4. Brush the remaining 1 tablespoon of the oil over the portabello mushroom caps. Place the mushrooms, bottom-side down, on the grill pan. Cover with a sheet of aluminum foil sprayed with nonstick cooking spray. Cook for 5 minutes.
5. Flip the mushroom caps over, and spoon about ½ cup of the cooked vegetable mixture into each cap. Top each with about 2½ tablespoons of the Mozzarella.
6. Cover and grill for 4 to 5 minutes, or until the cheese is melted.
7. Using a spatula, transfer the portabello mushrooms to a plate. Let cool for about 5 minutes before serving.

Nutrition Info:

- Info Per Serving: Calories: 111;Fat: 4.0g;Protein: 11.0g;Carbs: 11.0g.

Sweet Mustard Cabbage Hash

Servings:4
Cooking Time:30 Minutes
Ingredients:

- 1 head Savoy cabbage, shredded
- 3 tbsp olive oil
- 1 onion, finely chopped
- 2 garlic cloves, minced
- ½ tsp fennel seeds
- ¼ cup red wine vinegar
- 1 tbsp mustard powder
- 1 tbsp honey
- Salt and black pepper to taste

Directions:

1. Warm olive oil in a pan over medium heat and sauté onion, fennel seeds, cabbage, salt, and pepper for 8-9 minutes.

2. In a bowl, mix vinegar, mustard, and honey; set aside. Sauté garlic in the pan for 30 seconds. Pour in vinegar mixture and cook for 10-15 minutes until the liquid reduces by half.

Nutrition Info:

- Info Per Serving: Calories: 181;Fat: 12g;Protein: 3.4g;Carbs: 19g.

Grilled Za´atar Zucchini Rounds

Servings:4
Cooking Time:20 Minutes

Ingredients:

- 2 tbsp olive oil
- 4 zucchinis, sliced
- 1 tbsp za'atar seasoning
- Salt to taste
- 2 tbsp parsley, chopped

Directions:

1. Preheat the grill on high. Cut the zucchini lengthways into ½-inch thin pieces. Brush the zucchini 'steaks' with olive oil and season with salt and za'atar seasoning. Grill for 6 minutes on both sides. Sprinkle with parsley and serve.

Nutrition Info:

- Info Per Serving: Calories: 91;Fat: 7.4g;Protein: 2.4g;Carbs: 6.6g.

Potato Tortilla With Leeks And Mushrooms

Servings:2
Cooking Time: 50 Minutes

Ingredients:

- 1 tablespoon olive oil
- 1 cup thinly sliced leeks
- 4 ounces baby bella (cremini) mushrooms, stemmed and sliced
- 1 small potato, peeled and sliced ¼-inch thick
- 5 large eggs, beaten
- ½ cup unsweetened almond milk
- 1 teaspoon Dijon mustard
- ½ teaspoon dried thyme
- ½ teaspoon salt
- Pinch freshly ground black pepper
- 3 ounces Gruyère cheese, shredded

Directions:

1. Preheat the oven to 350ºF.

2. Heat the olive oil in a large sauté pan (nonstick is best) over medium-high heat. Add the leeks, mushrooms, and potato slices and sauté until the leeks are golden and the potatoes start to brown, about 10 minutes.

3. Reduce the heat to medium-low, cover, and let the vegetables cook for another 10 minutes, or until the potatoes begin to soften. If the potato slices stick to the bottom of the pan, add 1 to 2 tablespoons of water to the pan, but be careful because it may splatter.

4. Meanwhile, combine the beaten eggs, milk, mustard, thyme, salt, pepper, and cheese in a medium bowl and whisk everything together.

5. When the potatoes are soft enough to pierce with a fork or knife, turn off the heat.

6. Transfer the cooked vegetables to an oiled ovenproof pan (nonstick is best) and arrange them in a nice layer along the bottom and slightly up the sides of the pan.

7. Pour the egg mixture over the vegetables and give it a light shake or tap to distribute the eggs evenly through the vegetables.

8. Bake for 25 to 30 minutes, or until the eggs are set and the top is golden and puffed.

9. Remove from the oven and cool for 5 minutes before cutting and serving.

Nutrition Info:

- Info Per Serving: Calories: 541;Fat: 33.1g;Protein: 32.8g;Carbs: 31.0g.

Parsley & Olive Zucchini Bake

Servings:6
Cooking Time:1 Hour 40 Minutes

Ingredients:

- 3 tbsp olive oil
- 1 can tomatoes, diced
- 2 lb zucchinis, sliced
- 1 onion, chopped
- Salt and black pepper to taste
- 3 garlic cloves, minced
- ¼ tsp dried oregano
- ¼ tsp red pepper flakes
- 10 Kalamata olives, chopped
- 2 tbsp fresh parsley, chopped

Directions:

1. Preheat oven to 325 F. Warm the olive oil in a saucepan over medium heat. Sauté zucchini for about 3 minutes per side; transfer to a bowl. Stir-fry the onion and salt in the same saucepan for 3-5 minutes, stirring occasionally until

onion soft and lightly golden. Stir in garlic, oregano, and pepper flakes and cook until fragrant, about 30 seconds.

2. Add in olives, tomatoes, salt, and pepper, bring to a simmer, and cook for about 10 minutes, stirring occasionally. Return the zucchini, cover, and transfer the pot to the oven. Bake for 10-15 minutes. Sprinkle with parsley and serve.

Nutrition Info:

• Info Per Serving: Calories: 164;Fat: 6g;Protein: 1.5g;Carbs: 7.7g.

Tradicional Matchuba Green Beans

Servings:4
Cooking Time:15 Minutes
Ingredients:

• 1 ¼ lb narrow green beans, trimmed

• 3 tbsp butter, melted

• 1 cup Moroccan matbucha

• 2 green onions, chopped

• Salt and black pepper to taste

Directions:

1. Steam the green beans in a pot for 5-6 minutes until tender. Remove to a bowl, reserving the cooking liquid. In a skillet over medium heat, melt the butter. Add in green onions, salt, and black pepper and cook until fragrant. Lower the heat and put in the green beans along with some of the reserved water. Simmer for 3-4 minutes. Serve the green beans with the Sabra Moroccan matbucha as a dip.

Nutrition Info:

• Info Per Serving: Calories: 125;Fat: 8.6g;Protein: 2.2g;Carbs: 9g.

Fried Eggplant Rolls

Servings:4
Cooking Time: 10 Minutes
Ingredients:

• 2 large eggplants, trimmed and cut lengthwise into ¼-inch-thick slices

• 1 teaspoon salt

• 1 cup shredded ricotta cheese

• 4 ounces goat cheese, shredded

• ¼ cup finely chopped fresh basil

• ½ teaspoon freshly ground black pepper

• Olive oil spray

Directions:

1. Add the eggplant slices to a colander and season with salt. Set aside for 15 to 20 minutes.

2. Mix together the ricotta and goat cheese, basil, and black pepper in a large bowl and stir to combine. Set aside.

3. Dry the eggplant slices with paper towels and lightly mist them with olive oil spray.

4. Heat a large skillet over medium heat and lightly spray it with olive oil spray.

5. Arrange the eggplant slices in the skillet and fry each side for 3 minutes until golden brown.

6. Remove from the heat to a paper towel-lined plate and rest for 5 minutes.

7. Make the eggplant rolls: Lay the eggplant slices on a flat work surface and top each slice with a tablespoon of the prepared cheese mixture. Roll them up and serve immediately.

Nutrition Info:

• Info Per Serving: Calories: 254;Fat: 14.9g;Protein: 15.3g;Carbs: 18.6g.

Fish & Chickpea Stew

Servings:4
Cooking Time:30 Minutes
Ingredients:

• 3 tbsp olive oil

• 1 lb tilapia fish, cubed

• 1 lb canned chickpeas

• 1 cup canned tomatoes

• 1 parsnip, chopped

• 1 bell pepper, chopped

• ½ cup shallots, chopped

• 1 tsp garlic puree

• ½ tsp dried basil

• 1 bay leaf

• ¼ cup dry white wine

• 1 cup fish stock

• 2 cups vegetable broth

• Salt and black pepper to taste

Directions:

1. Warm the oil in a pot over medium heat. Add in parsnip, bell pepper, garlic, and shallots and cook for 3-5 minutes. Add in basil and bay leaf. Cook for another 30-40 seconds. Pour in white wine to scrape off any bits from the bottom.

2. Stir in fish stock, vegetable broth, and tomatoes. Bring to a boil, lower the heat, and simmer for 10 minutes. Mix in fish, chickpeas, salt, and black pepper. Simmer covered for 10 minutes more. Adjust the taste and discard the bay leaf.

Nutrition Info:

• Info Per Serving: Calories: 469;Fat: 13g;Protein: 34g;Carbs: 55g.

Cauliflower Steaks With Arugula

Servings:4
Cooking Time: 20 Minutes
Ingredients:
- Cauliflower:
- 1 head cauliflower
- Cooking spray
- ½ teaspoon garlic powder
- 4 cups arugula
- Dressing:
- 1½ tablespoons extra-virgin olive oil
- 1½ tablespoons honey mustard
- 1 teaspoon freshly squeezed lemon juice

Directions:
1. Preheat the oven to 425°F.
2. Remove the leaves from the cauliflower head, and cut it in half lengthwise. Cut 1½-inch-thick steaks from each half.
3. Spritz both sides of each steak with cooking spray and season both sides with the garlic powder.
4. Place the cauliflower steaks on a baking sheet, cover with foil, and roast in the oven for 10 minutes.
5. Remove the baking sheet from the oven and gently pull back the foil to avoid the steam. Flip the steaks, then roast uncovered for 10 minutes more.
6. Meanwhile, make the dressing: Whisk together the olive oil, honey mustard and lemon juice in a small bowl.
7. When the cauliflower steaks are done, divide into four equal portions. Top each portion with one-quarter of the arugula and dressing.
8. Serve immediately.
Nutrition Info:
- Info Per Serving: Calories: 115;Fat: 6.0g;Protein: 5.0g;Carbs: 14.0g.

Roasted Vegetables And Chickpeas

Servings:2
Cooking Time: 30 Minutes
Ingredients:
- 4 cups cauliflower florets (about ½ small head)
- 2 medium carrots, peeled, halved, and then sliced into quarters lengthwise
- 2 tablespoons olive oil, divided
- ½ teaspoon garlic powder, divided
- ½ teaspoon salt, divided

- 2 teaspoons za'atar spice mix, divided
- 1 can chickpeas, drained, rinsed, and patted dry
- ¾ cup plain Greek yogurt
- 1 teaspoon harissa spice paste

Directions:
1. Preheat the oven to 400°F. Line a sheet pan with foil or parchment paper.
2. Place the cauliflower and carrots in a large bowl. Drizzle with 1 tablespoon olive oil and sprinkle with ¼ teaspoon of garlic powder, ¼ teaspoon of salt, and 1 teaspoon of za'atar. Toss well to combine.
3. Spread the vegetables onto one half of the sheet pan in a single layer.
4. Place the chickpeas in the same bowl and season with the remaining 1 tablespoon of oil, ¼ teaspoon of garlic powder, and ¼ teaspoon of salt, and the remaining za'atar. Toss well to combine.
5. Spread the chickpeas onto the other half of the sheet pan.
6. Roast for 30 minutes, or until the vegetables are tender and the chickpeas start to turn golden. Flip the vegetables halfway through the cooking time, and give the chickpeas a stir so they cook evenly.
7. The chickpeas may need an extra few minutes if you like them crispy. If so, remove the vegetables and leave the chickpeas in until they're cooked to desired crispiness.
8. Meanwhile, combine the yogurt and harissa in a small bowl. Taste and add additional harissa as desired, then serve.
Nutrition Info:
- Info Per Serving: Calories: 468;Fat: 23.0g;Protein: 18.1g;Carbs: 54.1g.

Greek-style Eggplants

Servings:4
Cooking Time:25 Minutes
Ingredients:
- 1 ½ lb eggplants, sliced into rounds
- ¼ cup olive oil
- Salt and black pepper to taste
- 4 tsp balsamic vinegar
- 1 tbsp capers, minced
- 1 garlic clove, minced
- ½ tsp lemon zest
- ½ tsp fresh oregano, minced
- 3 tbsp fresh mint, minced
Directions:

1. Preheat oven to 420 F. Arrange the eggplant rounds on a greased baking dish and drizzle with some olive oil. Sprinkle with salt and pepper. Bake for 10-12 per side until mahogany lightly charred. Whisk remaining olive oil, balsamic vinegar, capers, garlic, lemon zest, oregano, salt, and pepper together in a bowl. Drizzle the mixture all over the eggplants and sprinkle with mint. Serve and enjoy!

Nutrition Info:

- Info Per Serving: Calories: 111;Fat: 9.2g;Protein: 1.2g;Carbs: 7g.

Mini Crustless Spinach Quiches

Servings:6

Cooking Time: 20 Minutes

Ingredients:

- 2 tablespoons extra-virgin olive oil
- 1 onion, finely chopped
- 2 cups baby spinach
- 2 garlic cloves, minced
- 8 large eggs, beaten
- ¼ cup unsweetened almond milk
- ½ teaspoon sea salt
- ¼ teaspoon freshly ground black pepper
- 1 cup shredded Swiss cheese
- Cooking spray

Directions:

1. Preheat the oven to 375ºF. Spritz a 6-cup muffin tin with cooking spray. Set aside.
2. In a large skillet over medium-high heat, heat the olive oil until shimmering. Add the onion and cook for about 4 minutes, or until soft. Add the spinach and cook for about 1 minute, stirring constantly, or until the spinach softens. Add the garlic and sauté for 30 seconds. Remove from the heat and let cool.
3. In a medium bowl, whisk together the eggs, milk, salt and pepper.
4. Stir the cooled vegetables and the cheese into the egg mixture. Spoon the mixture into the prepared muffin tins. Bake for about 15 minutes, or until the eggs are set.
5. Let rest for 5 minutes before serving.

Nutrition Info:

- Info Per Serving: Calories: 218;Fat: 17.0g;Protein: 14.0g;Carbs: 4.0g.

Artichoke & Bean Pot

Servings:4

Cooking Time:40 Minutes

Ingredients:

- 2 tbsp olive oil
- 10 artichoke hearts, halved
- 1 onion, sliced
- 12 whole baby carrots
- ½ cup chopped celery
- 1 lemon, juiced
- 2 tbsp chopped fresh basil
- 1 red chili, sliced
- ¾ cup frozen fava beans
- Salt and black pepper to taste

Directions:

1. Warm olive oil in a pot over medium heat and sauté onion, carrots, and celery for 7-8 minutes until tender. Stir in lemon juice, butter, and 1 cup of water. Bring to a boil, then lower the heat and simmer for 10-15 minutes. Add in artichoke hearts, fava beans, salt, and pepper and cook covered for another 10 minutes. Top with basil and red chili and serve.

Nutrition Info:

- Info Per Serving: Calories: 353;Fat: 4.1g;Protein: 22g;Carbs: 68g.

Baked Beet & Leek With Dilly Yogurt

Servings:4

Cooking Time:40 Minutes

Ingredients:

- 5 tbsp olive oil
- ½ lb leeks, thickly sliced
- 1 lb red beets, sliced
- 1 cup yogurt
- 2 garlic cloves, finely minced
- ¼ tsp cumin, ground
- ¼ tsp dried parsley
- ¼ cup parsley, chopped
- 1 tsp dill
- Salt and black pepper to taste

Directions:

1. Preheat the oven to 390 F. Arrange the beets and leeks on a greased roasting dish. Sprinkle with some olive oil, cumin, dried parsley, black pepper, and salt. Bake in the oven for 25-30 minutes. Transfer to a serving platter. In a bowl, stir in yogurt, dill, garlic, and the remaining olive oil.

Whisk to combine. Drizzle the veggies with the yogurt sauce and top with fresh parsley to serve.

Nutrition Info:

- Info Per Serving: Calories: 281;Fat: 18.7g;Protein: 5g;Carbs: 24g.

Cauliflower Cakes With Goat Cheese

Servings:4

Cooking Time:50 Minutes

Ingredients:

- ¼ cup olive oil
- 10 oz cauliflower florets
- 1 tsp ground turmeric
- 1 tsp ground coriander
- Salt and black pepper to taste
- ½ tsp ground mustard seeds
- 4 oz Goat cheese, softened
- 2 scallions, sliced thin
- 1 large egg, lightly beaten
- 2 garlic cloves, minced
- 1 tsp grated lemon zest
- 4 lemon wedges
- ¼ cup flour

Directions:

1. Preheat oven to 420 F. In a bowl, whisk 1 tablespoon oil, turmeric, coriander, salt, ground mustard, and pepper. Add in the cauliflower and toss to coat. Transfer to a greased baking sheet and spread it in a single layer. Roast for 20-25 minutes until cauliflower is well browned and tender. Transfer the cauliflower to a large bowl and mash it coarsely with a potato masher. Stir in Goat cheese, scallions, egg, garlic, and lemon zest until well combined. Sprinkle flour over cauliflower mixture and stir to incorporate. Shape the mixture into 10-12 cakes and place them on a sheet pan. Chill to firm, about 30 minutes. Warm the remaining olive oil in a skillet over medium heat. Fry the cakes for 5-6 minutes on each side until deep golden brown and crisp. Serve with lemon wedges.

Nutrition Info:

- Info Per Serving: Calories: 320;Fat: 25g;Protein: 13g;Carbs: 12g.

Brussels Sprouts Linguine

Servings:4

Cooking Time: 25 Minutes

Ingredients:

- 8 ounces whole-wheat linguine
- ⅓ cup plus 2 tablespoons extra-virgin olive oil, divided
- 1 medium sweet onion, diced
- 2 to 3 garlic cloves, smashed
- 8 ounces Brussels sprouts, chopped
- ½ cup chicken stock
- ⅓ cup dry white wine
- ½ cup shredded Parmesan cheese
- 1 lemon, quartered

Directions:

1. Bring a large pot of water to a boil and cook the pasta for about 5 minutes, or until al dente. Drain the pasta and reserve 1 cup of the pasta water. Mix the cooked pasta with 2 tablespoons of the olive oil. Set aside.

2. In a large skillet, heat the remaining ⅓ cup of the olive oil over medium heat. Add the onion to the skillet and sauté for about 4 minutes, or until tender. Add the smashed garlic cloves and sauté for 1 minute, or until fragrant.

3. Stir in the Brussels sprouts and cook covered for 10 minutes. Pour in the chicken stock to prevent burning. Once the Brussels sprouts have wilted and are fork-tender, add white wine and cook for about 5 minutes, or until reduced.

4. Add the pasta to the skillet and add the pasta water as needed.

5. Top with the Parmesan cheese and squeeze the lemon over the dish right before eating.

Nutrition Info:

- Info Per Serving: Calories: 502;Fat: 31.0g;Protein: 15.0g;Carbs: 50.0g.

Eggplant Rolls In Tomato Sauce

Servings:4

Cooking Time:60 Minutes

Ingredients:

- 2 tbsp olive oil
- 1 ½ cups ricotta cheese
- 2 cans diced tomatoes
- 1 shallot, finely chopped
- 2 garlic cloves, minced
- 1 tbsp Italian seasoning
- 1 tsp dried oregano
- 2 eggplants
- ½ cup grated mozzarella

- Salt to taste
- ¼ tsp red pepper flakes

Directions:

1. Preheat oven to 350 F. Warm olive oil in a pot over medium heat and sauté shallot and garlic for 3 minutes until tender and fragrant. Mix in tomatoes, oregano, Italian seasoning, salt, and red flakes and simmer for 6 minutes.

2. Cut the eggplants lengthwise into 1,5-inch slices and season with salt. Grill them for 2-3 minutes per side until softened. Place them on a plate and spoon 2 tbsp of ricotta cheese. Wrap them and arrange on a greased baking dish. Pour over the sauce and scatter with the mozzarella cheese. Bake for 15-20 minutes until golden-brown and bubbling.

Nutrition Info:

- Info Per Serving: Calories: 362;Fat: 17g;Protein: 19g;Carbs: 38g.

Roasted Vegetables

Servings:2

Cooking Time: 35 Minutes

Ingredients:

- 6 teaspoons extra-virgin olive oil, divided
- 12 to 15 Brussels sprouts, halved
- 1 medium sweet potato, peeled and cut into 2-inch cubes
- 2 cups fresh cauliflower florets
- 1 medium zucchini, cut into 1-inch rounds
- 1 red bell pepper, cut into 1-inch slices
- Salt, to taste

Directions:

1. Preheat the oven to 425ºF.

2. Add 2 teaspoons of olive oil, Brussels sprouts, sweet potato, and salt to a large bowl and toss until they are completely coated.

3. Transfer them to a large roasting pan and roast for 10 minutes, or until the Brussels sprouts are lightly browned.

4. Meantime, combine the cauliflower florets with 2 teaspoons of olive oil and salt in a separate bowl.

5. Remove from the oven. Add the cauliflower florets to the roasting pan and roast for 10 minutes more.

6. Meanwhile, toss the zucchini and bell pepper with the remaining olive oil in a medium bowl until well coated. Season with salt.

7. Remove the roasting pan from the oven and stir in the zucchini and bell pepper. Continue roasting for 15 minutes, or until the vegetables are fork-tender.

8. Divide the roasted vegetables between two plates and serve warm.

Nutrition Info:

- Info Per Serving: Calories: 333;Fat: 16.8g;Protein: 12.2g;Carbs: 37.6g.

Garlic-butter Asparagus With Parmesan

Servings:2

Cooking Time: 8 Minutes

Ingredients:

- 1 cup water
- 1 pound asparagus, trimmed
- 2 cloves garlic, chopped
- 3 tablespoons almond butter
- Salt and ground black pepper, to taste
- 3 tablespoons grated Parmesan cheese

Directions:

1. Pour the water into the Instant Pot and insert a trivet.

2. Put the asparagus on a tin foil add the butter and garlic. Season to taste with salt and pepper.

3. Fold over the foil and seal the asparagus inside so the foil doesn't come open. Arrange the asparagus on the trivet.

4. Secure the lid. Select the Manual mode and set the cooking time for 8 minutes at High Pressure.

5. Once cooking is complete, do a quick pressure release. Carefully open the lid.

6. Unwrap the foil packet and serve sprinkled with the Parmesan cheese.

Nutrition Info:

- Info Per Serving: Calories: 243;Fat: 15.7g;Protein: 12.3g;Carbs: 15.3g.

Parmesan Asparagus With Tomatoes

Servings:6

Cooking Time:30 Minutes

Ingredients:

- 3 tbsp olive oil
- 2 garlic cloves, minced
- 12 oz cherry tomatoes, halved
- 1 tsp dried oregano
- 10 Kalamata olives, chopped
- 2 lb asparagus, trimmed
- 2 tbsp fresh basil, chopped
- ¼ cup Parmesan cheese, grated
- Salt and black pepper to taste

Directions:

1. Warm 2 tbsp of olive oil in a skillet over medium heat sauté the garlic for 1-2 minutes, stirring often, until golden.

Add tomatoes, olives, and oregano and cook until tomatoes begin to break down, about 3 minutes; transfer to a bowl.

2. Coat the asparagus with the remaining olive oil and cook in a grill pan over medium heat for about 5 minutes, turning once until crisp-tender. Sprinkle with salt and pepper. Transfer asparagus to a serving platter, top with tomato mixture, and sprinkle with basil and Parmesan cheese. Serve and enjoy!

Nutrition Info:

• Info Per Serving: Calories: 157;Fat: 7g;Protein: 7.3g;Carbs: 19g.

Homemade Vegetarian Moussaka

Servings:4
Cooking Time:80 Minutes
Ingredients:

• 2 tbsp olive oil
• 1 yellow onion, chopped
• 2 garlic cloves, chopped
• 2 eggplants, halved
• ½ cup vegetable broth
• Salt and black pepper to taste
• ½ tsp paprika
• ¼ cup parsley, chopped
• 1 tsp basil, chopped
• 1 tsp hot sauce
• 1 tomato, chopped
• 2 tbsp tomato puree
• 6 Kalamata olives, chopped
• ½ cup feta cheese, crumbled

Directions:

1. Preheat oven to 360 F. Remove the tender center part of the eggplants and chop it. Arrange the eggplant halves on a baking tray and drizzle with some olive oil. Roast for 35-40 minutes.

2. Warm the remaining olive oil in a skillet over medium heat and add eggplant flesh, onion, and garlic and sauté for 5 minutes until tender. Stir in the vegetable broth, salt, pepper, basil, hot sauce, paprika, tomato, and tomato puree. Lower the heat and simmer for 10-15 minutes. Once the eggplants are ready, remove them from the oven and fill them with the mixture. Top with Kalamata olives and feta cheese. Return to the oven and bake for 10-15 minutes. Sprinkle with parsley.

Nutrition Info:

• Info Per Serving: Calories: 223;Fat: 14g;Protein: 5.9g;Carbs: 23g.

Creamy Cauliflower Chickpea Curry

Servings:4
Cooking Time: 15 Minutes
Ingredients:

• 3 cups fresh or frozen cauliflower florets
• 2 cups unsweetened almond milk
• 1 can low-sodium chickpeas, drained and rinsed
• 1 can coconut milk
• 1 tablespoon curry powder
• ¼ teaspoon garlic powder
• ¼ teaspoon ground ginger
• ⅛ teaspoon onion powder
• ¼ teaspoon salt

Directions:

1. Add the cauliflower florets, almond milk, chickpeas, coconut milk, curry powder, garlic powder, ginger, and onion powder to a large stockpot and stir to combine.

2. Cover and cook over medium-high heat for 10 minutes, stirring occasionally.

3. Reduce the heat to low and continue cooking uncovered for 5 minutes, or until the cauliflower is tender.

4. Sprinkle with the salt and stir well. Serve warm.

Nutrition Info:

• Info Per Serving: Calories: 409;Fat: 29.6g;Protein: 10.0g;Carbs: 29.8g.

Spinach & Lentil Stew

Servings:4
Cooking Time:40 Minutes
Ingredients:

• 2 tbsp olive oil
• 1 cup dry red lentils, rinsed
• 1 carrot, chopped
• 1 celery stalk, chopped
• 1 red onion, chopped
• 4 garlic cloves, minced
• 3 tomatoes, puréed
• 3 cups vegetable broth
• 1 tsp cayenne pepper
• ½ tsp ground cumin
• ½ tsp thyme
• 1 tsp turmeric
• 1 tbsp sweet paprika
• 1 cup spinach, chopped
• 1 cup fresh cilantro, chopped
• Salt and black pepper to taste

Directions:

1. Heat the olive oil in a pot over medium heat and sauté the garlic, carrot, celery, and onion until tender, about 4-5 minutes. Stir in cayenne pepper, cumin, thyme, paprika, and turmeric for 1 minute and add tomatoes; cook for 3 more minutes. Pour in vegetable broth and lentils and bring to a boil. Reduce the heat and simmer covered for 15 minutes. Stir in spinach and cook for 5 minutes until wilted. Adjust the seasoning and divide between bowls. Top with cilantro.

Nutrition Info:

- Info Per Serving: Calories: 310;Fat: 9g;Protein: 18.3g;Carbs: 41g.

Baked Vegetable Stew

Servings:6
Cooking Time:70 Minutes
Ingredients:

- 1 can diced tomatoes, drained with juice reserved
- 3 tbsp olive oil
- 1 onion, chopped
- 2 tbsp fresh oregano, minced
- 1 tsp paprika
- 4 garlic cloves, minced
- 1 ½ lb green beans, sliced
- 1 lb Yukon Gold potatoes, peeled and chopped
- 1 tbsp tomato paste
- Salt and black pepper to taste
- 3 tbsp fresh basil, chopped

Directions:

1. Preheat oven to 360 F. Warm the olive oil in a skillet over medium heat. Sauté onion and garlic for 3 minutes until softened. Stir in oregano and paprika for 30 seconds. Transfer to a baking dish and add in green beans, potatoes, tomatoes, tomato paste, salt, pepper, and 1 ½ cups of water; stir well. Bake for 40-50 minutes. Sprinkle with basil. Serve.

Nutrition Info:

- Info Per Serving: Calories: 121;Fat: 0.8g;Protein: 4.2g;Carbs: 26g.

Mushroom Filled Zucchini Boats

Servings:2
Cooking Time:50 Minutes
Ingredients:

- 2 zucchini, cut in half lengthwise
- 2 cups button mushrooms, chopped
- 2 tbsp olive oil
- 2 cloves garlic, minced

- 2 tbsp chicken broth
- ¼ tsp dried thyme
- 1 tbsp parsley, finely chopped
- 1 tbsp Italian seasoning
- Salt and black pepper to taste

Directions:

1. Preheat oven to 350 F. Warm the olive oil in a large skillet over medium heat and add the olive oil. Sauté the mushrooms and garlic for 4-5 minutes until tender. Pour in the chicken broth and cook for another 3–4 minutes. Add the parsley, oregano, and Italian seasoning and season with salt and pepper. Stir and remove from the heat. Spoon the mixture into the zucchini halves. Place them in a casserole dish and pour 2-3 tbsp of water or broth in the bottom. Cover with foil and bake for 30-40 minutes until zucchini is tender.

Nutrition Info:

- Info Per Serving: Calories: 165;Fat: 13.9g;Protein: 3.8g;Carbs: 8g.

Marinara Zoodles

Servings:4
Cooking Time:65 Minutes
Ingredients:

- 2 cans crushed tomatoes
- 2 tbsp olive oil
- 16 oz zucchini noodles
- 1 can diced tomatoes,
- 1 onion, chopped
- 4 garlic cloves, minced
- 1 tbsp dried Italian seasoning
- 1 tsp dried oregano
- Sea salt to taste
- ¼ tsp red pepper flakes
- ¼ cup Romano cheese, grated

Directions:

1. Warm olive oil in a pot over medium heat and sauté onion and garlic for 5 minutes, stirring frequently until fragrant. Pour in tomatoes, oregano, Italian seasoning, salt, and red pepper flakes. Bring just to a boil, then lower the heat, and simmer for 10-15 minutes. Stir in the zucchini noodles and cook for 3-4 minutes until the noodles are slightly softened. Scatter with Romano cheese and serve.

Nutrition Info:

- Info Per Serving: Calories: 209;Fat: 9g;Protein: 8.1g;Carbs: 27.8g.

Feta & Zucchini Rosti Cakes

Servings:4

Cooking Time:25 Minutes

Ingredients:

- 5 tbsp olive oil
- 1 lb zucchini, shredded
- 4 spring onions, chopped
- Salt and black pepper to taste
- 4 oz feta cheese, crumbled
- 1 egg, lightly beaten
- 2 tbsp minced fresh dill
- 1 garlic clove, minced
- ¼ cup flour
- Lemon wedges for serving

Directions:

1. Preheat oven to 380 F. In a large bowl, mix the zucchini, spring onions, feta cheese, egg, dill, garlic, salt, and pepper. Sprinkle flour over the mixture and stir to incorporate.

2. Warm the oil in a skillet over medium heat. Cook the rosti mixture in small flat fritters for about 4 minutes per side until crisp and golden on both sides, pressing with a fish slice as they cook. Serve with lemon wedges.

Nutrition Info:

- Info Per Serving: Calories: 239;Fat: 19.8g;Protein: 7.8g;Carbs: 9g.

Grilled Romaine Lettuce

Servings:4

Cooking Time: 3 To 5 Minutes

Ingredients:

- Romaine:
- 2 heads romaine lettuce, halved lengthwise
- 2 tablespoons extra-virgin olive oil
- Dressing:
- ½ cup unsweetened almond milk
- 1 tablespoon extra-virgin olive oil
- ¼ bunch fresh chives, thinly chopped
- 1 garlic clove, pressed
- 1 pinch red pepper flakes

Directions:

1. Heat a grill pan over medium heat.

2. Brush each lettuce half with the olive oil. Place the lettuce halves, flat-side down, on the grill. Grill for 3 to 5 minutes, or until the lettuce slightly wilts and develops light grill marks.

3. Meanwhile, whisk together all the ingredients for the dressing in a small bowl.

4. Drizzle 2 tablespoons of the dressing over each romaine half and serve.

Nutrition Info:

- Info Per Serving: Calories: 126;Fat: 11.0g;Protein: 2.0g;Carbs: 7.0g.

Baby Kale And Cabbage Salad

Servings:6

Cooking Time: 0 Minutes

Ingredients:

- 2 bunches baby kale, thinly sliced
- ½ head green savoy cabbage, cored and thinly sliced
- 1 medium red bell pepper, thinly sliced
- 1 garlic clove, thinly sliced
- 1 cup toasted peanuts
- Dressing:
- Juice of 1 lemon
- ¼ cup apple cider vinegar
- 1 teaspoon ground cumin
- ¼ teaspoon smoked paprika

Directions:

1. In a large mixing bowl, toss together the kale and cabbage.

2. Make the dressing: Whisk together the lemon juice, vinegar, cumin and paprika in a small bowl.

3. Pour the dressing over the greens and gently massage with your hands.

4. Add the pepper, garlic and peanuts to the mixing bowl. Toss to combine.

5. Serve immediately.

Nutrition Info:

- Info Per Serving: Calories: 199;Fat: 12.0g;Protein: 10.0g;Carbs: 17.0g.

Sides , Salads, And Soups Recipes

Mushroom & Spinach Orzo Soup

Servings:4
Cooking Time:20 Minutes
Ingredients:
- 2 tbsp butter
- 3 cups spinach
- ½ cup orzo
- 4 cups chicken broth
- 1 cup feta cheese, crumbled
- Salt and black pepper to taste
- ½ tsp dried oregano
- 1 onion, chopped
- 2 garlic cloves, minced
- 1 cup mushrooms, sliced

Directions:
1. Melt butter in a pot over medium heat and sauté onion, garlic, and mushrooms for 5 minutes until tender. Add in chicken broth, orzo, salt, pepper, and oregano. Bring to a boil and reduce the heat to a low. Continue simmering for 10 minutes, partially covered. Stir in spinach and continue to cook until the spinach wilts, about 3-4 minutes. Ladle into individual bowls and serve garnished with feta cheese.

Nutrition Info:
- Info Per Serving: Calories: 370;Fat: 11g;Protein: 23g;Carbs: 44g.

Chicken & Barley Soup

Servings:4
Cooking Time:40 Minutes
Ingredients:
- 2 tbsp olive oil
- 1 lb boneless chicken thighs
- ¼ cup pearl barley
- 1 red onion, chopped
- 2 cloves garlic, minced
- 4 cups chicken broth
- ¼ tsp oregano
- ½ lemon, juiced
- ¼ tsp parsley
- ¼ cup scallions, chopped
- Salt and black pepper to taste

Directions:

1. Heat the olive oil in a pot over medium heat and sweat the onion and garlic for 2-3 minutes until tender. Place in chicken thighs and cook for 5-6 minutes, stirring often.
2. Pour in chicken broth and barley and bring to a boil. Then lower the heat and simmer for 5 minutes. Remove the chicken and shred it with two forks. Return to the pot and add in lemon, oregano, and parsley. Simmer for 20-22 more minutes. Stir in shredded chicken and adjust the seasoning. Divide between 4 bowls and top with chopped scallions.

Nutrition Info:
- Info Per Serving: Calories: 373;Fat: 17g;Protein: 39g;Carbs: 14g.

Salmon & Curly Endive Salad

Servings:4
Cooking Time:5 Minutes
Ingredients:
- 4 oz smoked salmon, flaked
- 2 heads curly endive, torn
- 2 tsp yellow mustard
- ¼ cup lemon juice
- ½ cup Greek yogurt
- Salt and black pepper to taste
- 1 cucumber, sliced
- 2 tbsp chives, chopped

Directions:
1. Toss curly endive, salmon, mustard, lemon juice, yogurt, salt, pepper, cucumber, and chives in a bowl. Serve immediately.

Nutrition Info:
- Info Per Serving: Calories: 260;Fat: 18g;Protein: 17g;Carbs: 24g.

Cherry & Pine Nut Couscous

Servings:6
Cooking Time:10 Minutes
Ingredients:
- 2 tbsp olive oil
- 3 cups hot water
- 1 cup couscous
- ½ cup pine nuts, roasted
- ½ cup dry cherries, chopped
- ½ cup parsley, chopped
- Salt and black pepper to taste

1 tbsp lime juice

Directions:

1. Place couscous and hot water in a bowl and let sit for 10 minutes. Fluff with a fork and remove to a bowl. Stir in pine nuts, cherries, parsley, salt, pepper, lime juice, and olive oil.

Nutrition Info:

• Info Per Serving: Calories: 220;Fat: 8g;Protein: 5g;Carbs: 9g.

Effortless Bell Pepper Salad

Servings:4
Cooking Time:10 Minutes

Ingredients:

• 2 green bell peppers, cut into thick strips

• 2 red bell peppers, cut into thick strips

• 2 tbsp olive oil

• ½ cup feta cheese, crumbled

• Salt and black pepper to taste

Directions:

1. Combine bell peppers, olive oil, feta cheese, salt, and pepper in a bowl. Serve immediately.

Nutrition Info:

• Info Per Serving: Calories: 210;Fat: 6g;Protein: 4g;Carbs: 5g.

Cannellini Bean Stew With Spinach

Servings:4
Cooking Time:45 Minutes

Ingredients:

• 2 tbsp olive oil

• 1 onion, chopped

• 2 cloves garlic, minced

• 2 carrots, peeled and chopped

• 1 cup celery, chopped

• 4 cups vegetable broth

• 1 cup cannellini beans, soaked

• 1 tsp dried thyme

• 1 tsp dried rosemary

• 1 bay leaf

• 1 cup spinach, torn

• Salt and black pepper to taste

Directions:

1. Preheat your Instant Pot on Sauté mode and warm olive oil. Stir in garlic and onion, and cook for 3 minutes until tender and fragrant. Mix in celery and carrots and cook for 2 to 3 minutes more until they start to soften. Add broth,

bay leaf, thyme, rosemary, cannellini beans, and salt. Seal the lid and cook for 30 minutes on High Pressure. Do a quick pressure release. Stir in spinach and allow to sit for 2-4 minutes until the spinach wilts, and season with pepper and salt.

Nutrition Info:

• Info Per Serving: Calories: 285;Fat: 8.7g;Protein: 17g;Carbs: 36g.

Spinach & Bean Salad With Black Olives

Servings:4
Cooking Time:10 Minutes

Ingredients:

• ½ cup canned cannellini beans, drained

• 2 tbsp olive oil

• 2 cups baby spinach

• 1 cup black olives, halved

• 2 tbsp sunflower seeds

• 1 tbsp Dijon mustard

• 2 tbsp balsamic vinegar

Directions:

1. Combine beans, olive oil, spinach, olives, sunflower seeds, mustard, and vinegar in a bowl. Serve immediately.

Nutrition Info:

• Info Per Serving: Calories: 290;Fat: 7g;Protein: 13g;Carbs: 11g.

Horiatiki Salad (greek Salad)

Servings:4
Cooking Time:10 Minutes

Ingredients:

• 1 green bell pepper, cut into chunks

• 1 head romaine lettuce, torn

• ½ red onion, cut into rings

• 2 tomatoes, cut into wedges

• 1 cucumber, thinly sliced

• 3 tbsp extra-virgin olive oil

• 2 tbsp lemon juice

• Garlic salt and pepper to taste

• ¼ tsp dried Greek oregano

• 1 cup feta cheese, cubed

• 1 handful of Kalamata olives

Directions:

1. In a salad bowl, whisk the olive oil, lemon juice, pepper, garlic salt, and oregano. Add in the lettuce, red onion, tomatoes, cucumber, and bell pepper and mix with your

hands to coat. Top with feta and olives and serve immediately.

Nutrition Info:

- Info Per Serving: Calories: 226;Fat: 19g;Protein: 8g;Carbs: 9g.

Cucumber & Spelt Salad With Chicken

Servings:4

Cooking Time:35 Minutes

Ingredients:

- 4 tbsp olive oil
- ½ lb chicken breasts
- 1 tbsp dill, chopped
- 2 lemons, zested
- Juice of 2 lemons
- 3 tbsp parsley, chopped
- Salt and black pepper to taste
- 1 cup spelt grains
- 1 red leaf lettuce heads, torn
- 1 red onion, sliced
- 10 cherry tomatoes, halved
- 1 cucumber, sliced

Directions:

1. In a bowl, combine dill, lemon zest, lemon juice, 2 tbsp olive oil, parsley, salt, and pepper and mix well. Add in chicken breasts, toss to coat, cover, and refrigerate for 30 minutes. Place spelt grains in a pot and cover with water. Stir in salt and pepper. Put over medium heat and bring to a boil. Cook for 45 minutes and drain. Transfer to a bowl and let it cool.

2. Preheat the grill. Remove the chicken and grill for 12 minutes on all sides. Transfer to a bowl to cool before slicing. Once the spelt is cooled, add in the remaining olive oil, lettuce, onion, tomatoes, and cucumber and toss to coat. Top the salad with sliced chicken and serve.

Nutrition Info:

- Info Per Serving: Calories: 350;Fat: 18g;Protein: 27g;Carbs: 28g.

Moroccan Spiced Couscous

Servings:2

Cooking Time: 8 Minutes

Ingredients:

- 1 tablespoon olive oil
- ¾ cup couscous
- ¼ teaspoon cinnamon

- ¼ teaspoon garlic powder
- ¼ teaspoon salt, plus more as needed
- 1 cup water
- 2 tablespoons minced dried apricots
- 2 tablespoons raisins
- 2 teaspoons minced fresh parsley

Directions:

1. Heat the olive oil in a saucepan over medium-high heat until it shimmers.

2. Add the couscous, cinnamon, garlic powder, and salt. Stir for 1 minute to toast the couscous and spices.

3. Add the water, apricots, and raisins and bring the mixture to a boil.

4. Cover and turn off the heat. Allow the couscous to sit for 4 to 5 minutes and then fluff it with a fork. Sprinkle with the fresh parsley. Season with more salt as needed and serve.

Nutrition Info:

- Info Per Serving: Calories: 338;Fat: 8.0g;Protein: 9.0g;Carbs: 59.0g.

Moroccan Spinach & Lentil Soup

Servings:6

Cooking Time:35 Minutes

Ingredients:

- 3 tsp olive oil
- 1 onion, chopped
- 1 large carrot, chopped
- 3 garlic cloves, sliced
- 1 ½ cups lentils
- 1 cup crushed tomatoes
- 12 oz spinach

Directions:

1. Warm the olive oil and sauté the onion, garlic, and carrot for 3 minutes. Add the lentils, tomatoes, and 6 cups of water and stir. Cook until the lentils are tender, about 15-20 minutes. Add the spinach and stir until wilted, 5 minutes Serve hot.

Nutrition Info:

- Info Per Serving: Calories: 422;Fat: 17g;Protein: 22g;Carbs: 45g.

Pesto Ravioli Salad

Servings:6
Cooking Time:15 Minutes
Ingredients:

- 1 cup smoked mozzarella cheese, cubed
- ¼ tsp lemon zest
- 1 cup basil pesto
- ½ cup mayonnaise
- 2 red bell peppers, chopped
- 18 oz cheese ravioli

Directions:

1. Bring to a boil salted water in a pot over high heat. Add the ravioli and cook, uncovered, for 4-5 minutes, stirring occasionally; drain and place them in a salad bowl to cool slightly. Blend the lemon zest, pesto, and mayonnaise in a large bowl and stir in mozzarella cheese and bell peppers. Pour the mixture over the ravioli and toss to coat. Serve.

Nutrition Info:

- Info Per Serving: Calories: 447;Fat: 32g;Protein: 18g;Carbs: 24g.

Zesty Asparagus Salad

Servings:4
Cooking Time:10 Minutes
Ingredients:

- 4 tbsp olive oil
- 1 lb asparagus
- 1 garlic clove, minced
- Salt and black pepper to taste
- 1 tbsp balsamic vinegar
- 1 tbsp lemon zest

Directions:

1. Roast the asparagus in a greased skillet over medium heat for 5-6 minutes, turning once. Season to taste. Toss with garlic, olive oil, lemon zest, and vinegar. Serve.

Nutrition Info:

- Info Per Serving: Calories: 148;Fat: 13.6g;Protein: 8g;Carbs: 5.7g.

Anchovy Salad With Mustard Vinaigrette

Servings:6
Cooking Time:10 Minutes
Ingredients:

- ½ cup olive oil
- ½ lemon, juiced
- 1 tsp Dijon mustard
- ¼ tsp honey
- Salt and black pepper to taste
- 4 tomatoes, diced
- 1 cucumber, peeled and diced
- 1 lb arugula
- 1 red onion, thinly sliced
- 2 tbsp parsley, chopped
- 4 anchovy filets, chopped

Directions:

1. In a bowl, whisk together the olive oil, lemon juice, honey, and mustard, and season with salt and pepper. Set aside. In a separate bowl, combine all the vegetables with the parsley and toss. Add the sardine fillets on top of the salad. Drizzle the dressing over the salad just before serving.

Nutrition Info:

- Info Per Serving: Calories: 168;Fat: 6g;Protein: 8g;Carbs: 29g.

Quick Za´atar Spice

Servings:4
Cooking Time:5 Minutes
Ingredients:

- 1 tsp ground cumin
- 1 tsp ground coriander
- ½ cup dried thyme
- 2 tbsp sesame seeds, toasted
- 1 ½ tbsp ground sumac
- ¼ tsp Aleppo chili flakes

Directions:

1. Mix all the ingredients in a bowl. Store in a glass jar at room temperature for up to 7-9 months.

Nutrition Info:

- Info Per Serving: Calories: 175;Fat: 13.9g;Protein: 5g;Carbs: 12g.

Green Garden Salad

Servings:4
Cooking Time:10 Minutes
Ingredients:

- ¼ cup extra-virgin olive oil
- 2 green onions, sliced
- ½ tsp fresh lemon zest
- 3 tbsp balsamic vinegar
- Salt to taste
- 2 cups baby spinach
- 1 cup watercress
- 1 cup arugula
- 1 celery stick, sliced

Directions:

1. In a small bowl, whisk together the lemon zest, balsamic vinegar, olive oil, and salt. Put the remaining ingredients in a large bowl. Pour the dressing over the salad and lightly toss to coat. Serve and enjoy!

Nutrition Info:

- Info Per Serving: Calories: 172;Fat: 14g;Protein: 4.1g;Carbs: 9.8g.

Spanish Chorizo & Spicy Lentil Stew

Servings:6
Cooking Time:50 Minutes
Ingredients:

- 2 cups lentils
- 7 oz Spanish chorizo, chopped
- 1 onion, diced
- 2 garlic cloves, crushed
- 2 cups tomato sauce
- 2 cups vegetable broth
- ½ cup mustard
- ½ cup cider vinegar
- 3 tbsp Worcestershire sauce
- 2 tbsp maple syrup
- 2 tbsp liquid smoke
- 1 tbsp lime juice
- 2 cups brown sugar
- Salt and black pepper to taste
- 1 tsp chili powder
- 1 tsp paprika
- ¼ tsp cayenne pepper

Directions:

1. Preheat your Instant Pot on Sauté mode. Add in chorizo and cook for 3 minutes as you stir until crisp. Add garlic and onion and cook for 2 minutes until translucent. Mix the tomato sauce, broth, cider vinegar, liquid smoke, Worcestershire sauce, lime juice, mustard, and maple syrup in a mixing bowl. Pour the mixture into the pot to deglaze the pan, scraping the bottom of the pan to do away with any browned bits of food. Add pepper, chili, sugar, paprika, salt and cayenne into the sauce mixture as you stir to mix. Stir in lentils to coat. Seal the lid and cook on High Pressure for 30 minutes. Release pressure naturally for 10 minutes.

Nutrition Info:

- Info Per Serving: Calories: 692;Fat: 18g;Protein: 31g;Carbs: 104g.

Easy Roasted Cauliflower

Servings:2
Cooking Time: 20 Minutes
Ingredients:

- ½ large head cauliflower, stemmed and broken into florets
- 1 tablespoon olive oil
- 2 tablespoons freshly squeezed lemon juice
- 2 tablespoons tahini
- 1 teaspoon harissa paste
- Pinch salt

Directions:

1. Preheat the oven to 400ºF. Line a sheet pan with parchment paper.
2. Toss the cauliflower florets with the olive oil in a large bowl and transfer to the sheet pan.
3. Roast in the preheated oven for 15 minutes, flipping the cauliflower once or twice, or until it starts to become golden.
4. Meanwhile, in a separate bowl, combine the lemon juice, tahini, harissa, and salt and stir to mix well.
5. Remove the pan from the oven and toss the cauliflower with the lemon tahini sauce. Return to the oven and roast for another 5 minutes. Serve hot.

Nutrition Info:

- Info Per Serving: Calories: 205;Fat: 15.0g;Protein: 4.0g;Carbs: 15.0g.

Hearty Veggie Slaw

Servings:4
Cooking Time: 0 Minutes
Ingredients:
- Salad:
- 2 large broccoli stems, peeled and shredded
- ½ celery root bulb, peeled and shredded
- ¼ cup chopped fresh Italian parsley
- 1 large beet, peeled and shredded
- 2 carrots, peeled and shredded
- 1 small red onion, sliced thin
- 2 zucchinis, shredded
- Dressing:
- 1 teaspoon Dijon mustard
- ½ cup apple cider vinegar
- 1 tablespoon raw honey
- 1 teaspoon sea salt
- ¼ teaspoon freshly ground black pepper
- 2 tablespoons extra-virgin olive oil
- Topping:
- ½ cup crumbled feta cheese

Directions:
1. Combine the ingredients for the salad in a large salad bowl, then toss to combine well.
2. Combine the ingredients for the dressing in a small bowl, then stir to mix well.
3. Dressing the salad, then serve with feta cheese on top.

Nutrition Info:
Info Per Serving: Calories: 387;Fat: 30.2g;Protein: .1g;Carbs: 25.9g.

Bean & Endive Salad With Cucumber

Servings:4
Cooking Time:10 Minutes
Ingredients:
- 15 oz canned great northern beans
- 2 tbsp olive oil
- 2 tomatoes, cubed
- 2 endive heads, sliced
- 1 cucumber, sliced
- 1 tbsp parsley, chopped
- Salt and black pepper to taste
- 2 tbsp balsamic vinegar

Directions:
1. Combine beans, olive oil, endive, cucumber, parsley, tomatoes, salt, pepper, and vinegar in a bowl. Serve chilled.

Nutrition Info:
- Info Per Serving: Calories: 250;Fat: 10g;Protein: 9g;Carbs: 14g.

Chili Lentil Soup

Servings:4
Cooking Time:30 Minutes
Ingredients:
- 2 tbsp olive oil
- 1 cup lentils, rinsed
- 1 onion, chopped
- 2 carrots, chopped
- 1 potato, cubed
- 1 tomato, chopped
- 4 garlic cloves, minced
- 4 cups vegetable broth
- ½ tsp chili powder
- Salt and black pepper to taste
- 2 tbsp fresh parsley, chopped

Directions:
1. Warm the olive oil in a pot over medium heat. Add in onion, garlic, and carrots and sauté for 5-6 minutes until tender. Mix in lentils, broth, salt, pepper, chili powder, potato, and tomato. Bring to a boil, lower the heat and simmer for 15-18 minutes, stirring often. Top with parsley and serve.

Nutrition Info:
- Info Per Serving: Calories: 331;Fat: 9g;Protein: 19g;Carbs: 44.3g.

Classic Potato Salad With Green Onions

Servings:4
Cooking Time:25 Minutes
Ingredients:
- 2 ½ lb baby potatoes, halved
- Salt and black pepper to taste
- 1 cup light mayonnaise
- Juice of 1 lemon
- 2 green onions, chopped
- ¼ cup parsley, chopped

Directions:
1. Place potatoes and enough water in a pot over medium heat and bring to a boil. Cook for 12 minutes and drain; set aside.
2. In a bowl, mix mayonnaise, salt, pepper, lemon juice, and green onions. Add in the baby potatoes and toss to coat. Top with parsley and serve immediately.

Nutrition Info:

49

- Info Per Serving: Calories: 360;Fat: 20g;Protein: 11g;Carbs: 25g.

Lamb & Spinach Soup

Servings:4
Cooking Time:60 Minutes
Ingredients:

- ½ lb lamb shoulder, cut into bite-sized pieces
- 2 tbsp olive oil
- 1 onion, chopped
- 2 garlic cloves, minced
- 10 oz spinach, chopped
- 4 cups vegetable broth
- Salt and black pepper to taste

Directions:

1. Warm the olive oil on Sauté in your Instant Pot. Sauté the lamb, onion, and garlic for 6-8 minutes, stirring often. Pour in the broth and adjust the seasoning with salt and pepper. Seal the lid, press Soup/Broth, and cook for 30 minutes on High Pressure. Do a natural pressure release for 10 minutes. Press Sauté and add the spinach. Cook for 5 minutes. Serve.

Nutrition Info:

- Info Per Serving: Calories: 188;Fat: 12g;Protein: 14g;Carbs: 9g.

Basil Zucchini Marinara

Servings:4
Cooking Time:25 Minutes
Ingredients:

- 2 tbsp olive oil
- 1 shallot, chopped
- 1 garlic clove, minced
- 1 zucchini, sliced into rounds
- Salt and black pepper to taste
- 1 cup marinara sauce
- ¼ cup mozzarella, shredded
- 2 tbsp fresh basil, chopped

Directions:

1. Warm the olive oil in a skillet over medium heat. Sauté the shallot and garlic for 3 minutes until just tender and fragrant. Add in the zucchini and season with salt and pepper; cook for 4 minutes until lightly browned. Add marinara sauce and bring to a simmer; cook until zucchini is tender, 5-8 minutes. Scatter the mozzarella cheese on top of the zucchini layer and cover; heat for about 3 minutes until the cheese is melted. Sprinkle with basil and serve immediately.

Nutrition Info:

- Info Per Serving: Calories: 93;Fat: 7g;Protein: 3g;Carbs 5g.

Goat Cheese & Beet Salad With Nuts

Servings:4
Cooking Time:10 Minutes
Ingredients:

- 3 steamed beets, cut into wedges
- 3 tbsp olive oil
- Salt and black pepper to taste
- 2 tbsp lime juice
- 4 oz goat cheese, crumbled
- 1/3 cup hazelnuts, chopped
- 1 tbsp chives, chopped

Directions:

1. Heat a pan over medium heat and toast the hazelnuts for 1-2 minutes, shaking the pan often. Remove and let cool
2. In a bowl, mix olive oil, lime juice, salt, and pepper Arrange beets on a serving platter. Drizzle with the dressing Sprinkle with goat cheese, hazelnuts, and chives and serve.

Nutrition Info:

- Info Per Serving: Calories: 160;Fat: 5g;Protein 5g;Carbs: 7g.

Mushroom Sauce

Servings:4
Cooking Time:15 Minutes
Ingredients:

- 1 cup cremini mushrooms, chopped
- 2 tbsp olive oil
- 1 small onion, chopped
- 2 garlic cloves, minced
- 3 tbsp butter
- ½ cup white wine
- ½ cup vegetable broth
- 1 cup heavy cream
- 2 tbsp parsley, chopped

Directions:

1. Heat the olive oil in a pan over medium. Add the onion and garlic and sauté until the onion is translucent, 3 minutes Add the butter and mushrooms and cook for 5-7 minutes until the mushrooms are tender. Pour in the wine and scrape up any browned bits from the bottom of the pan. Simmer for 3-4 minutes. Add the vegetable broth and simmer for minutes until the sauce reduces by about three quarters Add the heavy cream and simmer for 2-3 minutes. Sprinkle with parsley. Serve and enjoy!

Nutrition Info:

Info Per Serving: Calories: 283;Fat: 27g;Protein: 2.1g;Carbs: 5g.

Whipped Feta Spread

Servings:6
Cooking Time:10 Minutes
Ingredients:
- 4 tbsp Greek yogurt
- ½ lb feta cheese, crumbled
- 3 cloves garlic, pressed
- 2 tbsp extra-virgin olive oil
- 2 tbsp finely chopped dill
- 1 tsp dried oregano
- Black pepper to taste

Directions:
1. Combine feta, yogurt, garlic, olive oil, and oregano in your food processor. Pulse until well combined. Keep in the fridge until required. To serve, spoon into a dish and sprinkle with dill and black pepper.

Nutrition Info:
- Info Per Serving: Calories: 155;Fat: 13g;Protein: g;Carbs: 4g.

Chilled Soup With Prawns

Servings:4
Cooking Time:15 Minutes
Ingredients:
- 1 lb prawns, peeled and deveined
- 3 tbsp olive oil
- 1 cucumber, chopped
- 3 cups tomato juice
- 3 roasted red peppers, chopped
- 2 tbsp balsamic vinegar
- 1 garlic clove, minced
- Salt and black pepper to taste
- ½ tsp cumin
- 1 tsp thyme, chopped

Directions:
. In a food processor, blitz tomato juice, cucumber, red peppers, 2 tbsp of olive oil, vinegar, cumin, salt, pepper, and garlic until smooth. Remove to a bowl and transfer to the fridge for 10 minutes. Warm the remaining oil in a pot over medium heat and sauté prawns, salt, pepper, and thyme for 4 minutes on all sides. Let cool. Ladle the soup into individual bowls and serve topped with prawns.

Nutrition Info:
Info Per Serving: Calories: 270;Fat: 12g;Protein: g;Carbs: 13g.

Summer Gazpacho

Servings:6
Cooking Time:15 Minutes
Ingredients:
- ⅓ cup extra-virgin olive oil
- ½ cup of water
- 2 bread slices, torn
- 2 lb ripe tomatoes, seeded
- 1 cucumber, chopped
- 1 clove garlic, finely chopped
- ½ red onion, diced
- 2 tbsp red wine vinegar
- 1 tbsp fresh thyme, chopped
- Salt to taste

Directions:
1. Put the bread in 1 cup of water mixed with 1 tbsp of vinegar and salt to soak for 5 minutes. Then, blend the soaked bread, tomatoes, cucumber, garlic, red onion, olive oil, vinegar, thyme, and salt in your food processor until completely smooth. Pour the soup into a glass container and store in the fridge until chilled. Serve drizzled with olive oil.

Nutrition Info:
- Info Per Serving: Calories: 163;Fat: 13g;Protein: 2g;Carbs: 12.4g.

Cumin Cauli Mash

Servings:4
Cooking Time:25 Minutes
Ingredients:
- 2 tbsp butter
- ¼ cup grated Parmesan cheese
- 4 cups cauliflower florets
- ¼ cup milk
- 2 tbsp wholegrain mustard
- 1 tsp ground cumin
- 1 tsp crushed chilies
- Salt and black pepper to taste

Directions:
1. Boil the cauliflower in a pot of salted water for 10 minutes. Drain and place in a large bowl. Add in milk, butter, cheese, mustard, cumin, salt, and pepper. Mash until smooth with a potato masher. Top with crushed chilies and serve.

Nutrition Info:
- Info Per Serving: Calories: 117;Fat: 8g;Protein: 4.6g;Carbs: 8.3g.

Beans , Grains, And Pastas Recipes

Israeli Style Eggplant And Chickpea Salad

Servings:6

Cooking Time: 20 Minutes

Ingredients:

- 2 tablespoons balsamic vinegar
- 2 tablespoons freshly squeezed lemon juice
- 1 teaspoon ground cumin
- ¼ teaspoon sea salt
- 2 tablespoons olive oil, divided
- 1 medium globe eggplant, stem removed, cut into flat cubes (about ½ inch thick)
- 1 can chickpeas, drained and rinsed
- ¼ cup chopped mint leaves
- 1 cup sliced sweet onion
- 1 garlic clove, finely minced
- 1 tablespoon sesame seeds, toasted

Directions:

1. Preheat the oven to 550ºF or the highest level of your oven or broiler. Grease a baking sheet with 1 tablespoon of olive oil.

2. Combine the balsamic vinegar, lemon juice, cumin, salt, and 1 tablespoon of olive oil in a small bowl. Stir to mix well.

3. Arrange the eggplant cubes on the baking sheet, then brush with 2 tablespoons of the balsamic vinegar mixture on both sides.

4. Broil in the preheated oven for 8 minutes or until lightly browned. Flip the cubes halfway through the cooking time.

5. Meanwhile, combine the chickpeas, mint, onion, garlic, and sesame seeds in a large serving bowl. Drizzle with remaining balsamic vinegar mixture. Stir to mix well.

6. Remove the eggplant from the oven. Allow to cool for 5 minutes, then slice them into ½-inch strips on a clean work surface.

7. Add the eggplant strips in the serving bowl, then toss to combine well before serving.

Nutrition Info:

- Info Per Serving: Calories: 125;Fat: 2.9g;Protein: 5.2g;Carbs: 20.9g.

Classic Falafel

Servings:6

Cooking Time:20 Minutes

Ingredients:

- 2 cups olive oil
- Salt and black pepper to taste
- 1 cup chickpeas, soaked
- 5 scallions, chopped
- ¼ cup fresh parsley leaves
- ¼ cup fresh cilantro leaves
- ¼ cup fresh dill
- 6 garlic cloves, minced
- ½ tsp ground cumin
- ½ tsp ground coriander

Directions:

1. Pat dry chickpeas with paper towels and place them in your food processor. Add in scallions, parsley, cilantro, dill garlic, salt, pepper, cumin, and ground coriander and pulse scraping downsides of the bowl as needed. Shape the chickpea mixture into 2-tablespoon-size disks, about 1 ½ inches wide and 1 inch thick, and place on a parchment paper–lined baking sheet.

2. Warm the olive oil in a skillet over medium heat. Fry the falafel until deep golden brown, 2-3 minutes per side. With a slotted spoon, transfer falafel to a paper towel-lined plate to drain. Serve hot.

Nutrition Info:

- Info Per Serving: Calories: 349;Fat: 26.3g;Protein 19g;Carbs: 9g.

Parmesan Polenta

Servings:6

Cooking Time:50 Minutes

Ingredients:

- 1 ½ cups coarse-ground cornmeal
- 2 tbsp olive oil
- 6 ½ cups water
- Salt and black pepper to taste
- ½ tsp baking soda
- 2 oz Pecorino cheese, grated

Directions:

1. In a large saucepan, bring water to a boil over medium heat. Stir in 1 teaspoon of salt and baking soda. Slowly pour cornmeal into water in a steady stream while stirring back

nd forth with a wooden spoon or rubber spatula. Bring mixture to boil, stirring constantly, about 1 minute. Reduce heat to the lowest setting and cover. After 4 minutes, whisk polenta to smooth out any lumps that may have formed, about 20 seconds. Cover and continue to cook, without stirring, until polenta grains are tender but slightly al dente, about 23 minutes longer. Off heat, stir in Pecorino and oil and season with pepper to taste. Cover and let sit for 5 minutes. Serve along with extra Pecorino cheese on the side.

Nutrition Info:

- Info Per Serving: Calories: 235;Fat: 18g;Protein: 1g;Carbs: 29g.

Cheesy Sage Farro

Servings:4
Cooking Time:50 Minutes
Ingredients:

- 2 tbsp olive oil
- 1 cup farro
- 1 red onion, chopped
- 5 sage leaves
- 1 garlic clove, minced
- 1 tbsp Parmesan cheese, grated
- 6 cups veggie stock
- Salt and black pepper to taste

Directions:

1. Warm the olive oil in a skillet over medium heat and cook onion and garlic for 5 minutes. Stir in sage leaves, faro, veggie stock, salt, and pepper and bring to a simmer. Cook for 40 minutes. Mix in Parmesan cheese and serve.

Nutrition Info:

- Info Per Serving: Calories: 220;Fat: 7.1g;Protein: g;Carbs: 8.9g.

Quinoa & Watercress Salad With Nuts

Servings:4
Cooking Time:5 Minutes
Ingredients:

- 2 boiled eggs, cut into wedges
- 2 cups watercress
- 2 cups cherry tomatoes, halved
- 1 cucumber, sliced
- 1 cup quinoa, cooked
- 1 cup almonds, chopped
- 2 tbsp olive oil
- 1 avocado, peeled and sliced

- 2 tbsp fresh cilantro, chopped
- Salt to taste
- 1 lemon, juiced

Directions:

1. Place watercress, cherry tomatoes, cucumber, quinoa, almonds, olive oil, cilantro, salt, and lemon juice in a bowl and toss to combine. Top with egg wedges and avocado slices and serve immediately.

Nutrition Info:

- Info Per Serving: Calories: 530;Fat: 35g;Protein: 20g;Carbs: 45g.

Traditional Beef Lasagna

Servings:4
Cooking Time:70 Minutes
Ingredients:

- 2 tbsp olive oil
- 1 lb lasagne sheets
- 1 lb ground beef
- 1 white onion, chopped
- 1 tsp Italian seasoning
- Salt and black pepper to taste
- 1 cup marinara sauce
- ½ cup grated Parmesan cheese

Directions:

1. Preheat oven to 350 F. Warm olive oil in a skillet and add the beef and onion. Cook until the beef is brown, 7-8 minutes. Season with Italian seasoning, salt, and pepper. Cook for 1 minute and mix in the marinara sauce. Simmer for 3 minutes.

2. Spread a layer of the beef mixture in a lightly greased baking sheet and make a first single layer on the beef mixture. Top with a single layer of lasagna sheets. Repeat the layering two more times using the remaining ingredients in the same quantities. Sprinkle with Parmesan cheese. Bake in the oven until the cheese melts and is bubbly with the sauce, 20 minutes. Remove the lasagna, allow cooling for 2 minutes and dish onto serving plates. Serve warm.

Nutrition Info:

- Info Per Serving: Calories: 557;Fat: 29g;Protein: 60g;Carbs: 4g.

Turkish Canned Pinto Bean Salad

Servings:4

Cooking Time: 3 Minutes

Ingredients:

- ¼ cup extra-virgin olive oil, divided
- 3 garlic cloves, lightly crushed and peeled
- 2 cans pinto beans, rinsed
- 2 cups plus 1 tablespoon water
- Salt and pepper, to taste
- ¼ cup tahini
- 3 tablespoons lemon juice
- 1 tablespoon ground dried Aleppo pepper, plus extra for serving
- 8 ounces cherry tomatoes, halved
- ¼ red onion, sliced thinly
- ½ cup fresh parsley leaves
- 2 hard-cooked large eggs, quartered
- 1 tablespoon toasted sesame seeds

Directions:

1. Add 1 tablespoon of the olive oil and garlic to a medium saucepan over medium heat. Cook for about 3 minutes, stirring constantly, or until the garlic turns golden but not brown.

2. Add the beans, 2 cups of the water and 1 teaspoon salt and bring to a simmer. Remove from the heat, cover and let sit for 20 minutes. Drain the beans and discard the garlic.

3. In a large bowl, whisk together the remaining 3 tablespoons of the oil, tahini, lemon juice, Aleppo, the remaining 1 tablespoon of the water and ¼ teaspoon salt. Stir in the beans, tomatoes, onion and parsley. Season with salt and pepper to taste.

4. Transfer to a serving platter and top with the eggs. Sprinkle with the sesame seeds and extra Aleppo before serving.

Nutrition Info:

- Info Per Serving: Calories: 402;Fat: 18.9g;Protein: 16.2g;Carbs: 44.4g.

Moroccan-style Vegetable Bean Stew

Servings:6

Cooking Time:50 Minutes

Ingredients:

- 3 tbsp olive oil
- 1 onion, chopped
- 8 oz Swiss chard, torn
- 4 garlic cloves, minced
- 1 tsp ground cumin
- ½ tsp paprika
- ½ tsp ground coriander
- ¼ tsp ground cinnamon
- 2 tbsp tomato paste
- 2 tbsp cornstarch
- 4 cups vegetable broth
- 2 carrots, chopped
- 1 can chickpeas
- 1 can butter beans
- 3 tbsp minced fresh parsley
- 3 tbsp harissa sauce
- Salt and black pepper to taste

Directions:

1. Warm the olive oil in a saucepan over medium heat. Sauté the onion until softened, about 3 minutes. Stir in garlic, cumin, paprika, coriander, and cinnamon and cook until fragrant, about 30 seconds. Stir in tomato paste and cornstarch and cook for 1 minute. Pour in broth and carrots, scraping up any browned bits, smoothing out any lumps, and bringing to boil. Reduce to a gentle simmer and cook for 10 minutes. Stir in chard, chickpeas, beans, salt, and pepper and simmer until vegetables are tender, 10-15 minutes. Sprinkle with parsley and some harissa sauce. Serve with the remaining sauce harissa on the side.

Nutrition Info:

- Info Per Serving: Calories: 387;Fat: 3.2g;Protein: 7g;Carbs: 28.7g.

Portuguese Thyme & Mushroom Millet

Servings:6

Cooking Time:35 Minutes

Ingredients:

- 10 oz cremini mushrooms, chopped
- 3 tbsp olive oil
- 1 ½ cups millet
- Salt and black pepper to taste
- 1 shallot, minced
- ½ tsp dried thyme
- 3 tbsp dry sherry
- 3 tbsp parsley, minced
- 1 ½ tsp Port wine

Directions:

1. In a large pot, bring 4 quarts of water to a boil. Add millet and a pinch of salt, return to a boil and cook until tender, 15-20 minutes. Drain millet and cover to keep warm.

2. Warm 2 tablespoons of oil in a large skillet over medium heat. Add mushrooms, shallot, thyme, and salt and stir occasionally, until moisture has evaporated and vegetables start to brown, 10 minutes. Stir in wine, scraping off any browned bits from the bottom until the skillet is almost dry. Add the remaining oil and farro and keep stirring for 2 minutes. Stir in parsley and wine. Season with salt and pepper and serve.

Nutrition Info:

- Info Per Serving: Calories: 323;Fat: 18g;Protein: 0g;Carbs: 27g.

Mushroom Bulgur Pilaf With Almonds

Servings:2

Cooking Time:45 Minutes

Ingredients:

- 3 scallions, minced
- 2 oz mushrooms, sliced
- 1 tbsp olive oil
- 1 garlic clove, minced
- ¼ cup almonds, sliced
- ½ cup bulgur
- 1 ½ cups chicken stock
- ½ tsp dried thyme
- 1 tbsp parsley, chopped
- Salt to taste

Directions:

1. Warm the olive oil in a saucepan over medium heat. Add garlic, scallions, mushrooms, and almonds, and sauté for 3 minutes. Pour the bulgur and cook, stirring, for 1 minute to toast it. Add the stock and thyme and bring the mixture to a boil. Cover and reduce the heat to low. Simmer the bulgur for 25 minutes or until the liquid is absorbed and the bulgur is tender. Sprinkle with parsley and season with salt to serve.

Nutrition Info:

- Info Per Serving: Calories: 342;Fat: 15g;Protein: 11g;Carbs: 48g.

Pea & Mint Tortellini

Servings:4

Cooking Time:30 Minutes

Ingredients:

- 1 package frozen cheese tortellini
- 2 tbsp olive oil
- 3 garlic cloves, minced
- ½ cup vegetable broth
- 2 cups frozen baby peas
- 1 lemon, zested
- 2 tbsp mint leaves, chopped

Directions:

1. Bring to a boil salted water in a pot over high heat. Add the tortellini and cook according to package directions. Drain and transfer to a bowl. Warm the olive oil in a large saucepan over medium and sauté the garlic for 2 minutes until golden. Pour in the broth and peas and bring to a simmer. Add in the tortellini and cook for 4–5 minutes until the mixture is slightly thickened. Stir in lemon zest, top with mint, and serve.

Nutrition Info:

- Info Per Serving: Calories: 272;Fat: 11g;Protein: 11g;Carbs: 34g.

Spinach & Salmon Fettuccine In White Sauce

Servings:4
Cooking Time:35 Minutes
Ingredients:

- 5 tbsp butter
- 16 oz fettuccine
- 4 salmon fillets, cubed
- Salt and black pepper to taste
- 3 garlic cloves, minced
- 1 ¼ cups heavy cream
- ½ cup dry white wine
- 1 tsp grated lemon zest
- 1 cup baby spinach
- Lemon wedges for garnishing

Directions:

1. In a pot of boiling water, cook the fettuccine pasta for 8-10 minutes until al dente. Drain and set aside.

2. Melt half of the butter in a large skillet; season the salmon with salt, black pepper, and cook in the butter until golden brown on all sides and flaky within, 8 minutes. Transfer to a plate and set aside.

3. Add the remaining butter to the skillet to melt and stir in the garlic. Cook until fragrant, 1 minute. Mix in heavy cream, white wine, lemon zest, salt, and pepper. Allow boiling over low heat for 5 minutes. Stir in spinach, allow wilting for 2 minutes and stir in fettuccine and salmon until well-coated in the sauce. Garnish with lemon wedges.

Nutrition Info:

- Info Per Serving: Calories: 795;Fat: 46g;Protein: 72g;Carbs: 20g.

Bean & Egg Noodles With Lemon Sauce

Servings:4
Cooking Time:20 Minutes
Ingredients:

- 3 tbsp olive oil
- 12 oz egg noodles
- 1 can diced tomatoes
- 1 can cannellini beans
- ½ cup heavy cream
- 1 cup vegetable stock
- 2 garlic cloves, minced
- 1 onion, chopped
- 1 cup spinach, chopped

- 1 tsp dill
- 1 tsp thyme
- ½ tsp red pepper, crushed
- 1 tsp lemon juice
- 1 tbsp fresh basil, chopped

Directions:

1. Warm the olive oil in a pot over medium heat. Add in onion and garlic and cook for 3 minutes until softened. Stir in dill, thyme, and red pepper for 1 minute. Add in spinach, vegetable stock, and tomatoes. Bring to a boil, add the egg noodles, cover, and lower the heat. Cook for 5-7 minutes. Put in beans and cook until heated through. Combine the heavy cream, lemon juice, and basil. Serve the dish with creamy lemon sauce on the side.

Nutrition Info:

- Info Per Serving: Calories: 641;Fat: 19g;Protein: 28g;Carbs: 92g.

Authentic Fettuccine A La Puttanesca

Servings:4
Cooking Time:20 Minutes
Ingredients:

- 2 tbsp extra-virgin olive oil
- 20 Kalamata olives, chopped
- ¼ cup fresh basil, chopped
- 4 garlic cloves, minced
- 2 anchovy fillets, chopped
- ¼ tsp red pepper flakes
- 3 tbsp capers
- 3 cans diced tomatoes
- 8 oz fettuccine pasta
- 2 tbsp Parmesan cheese, grated
- Salt and black pepper to taste

Directions:

1. Cook the fettuccine pasta according to pack instructions, drain and let it to cool. Warm olive oil in a skillet over medium heat and cook garlic and red flakes for 2 minutes. Add in capers, anchovies, olives, salt, and pepper and cook for another 2-3 minutes until the anchovies melt into the oil. Blend tomatoes in a food processor. Pour into the skillet and stir-fry for 5 minutes. Mix in basil and pasta. Serve garnished with Parmesan cheese.

Nutrition Info:

- Info Per Serving: Calories: 443;Fat: 14g;Protein: 18g;Carbs: 65g.

Papaya, Jicama, And Peas Rice Bowl

Servings:4
Cooking Time: 45 Minutes
Ingredients:
- Sauce:
- Juice of ¼ lemon
- 2 teaspoons chopped fresh basil
- 1 tablespoon raw honey
- 1 tablespoon extra-virgin olive oil
- Sea salt, to taste
- Rice:
- 1½ cups wild rice
- 2 papayas, peeled, seeded, and diced
- 1 jicama, peeled and shredded
- 1 cup snow peas, julienned
- 2 cups shredded cabbage
- 1 scallion, white and green parts, chopped

Directions:
1. Combine the ingredients for the sauce in a bowl. Stir to mix well. Set aside until ready to use.
2. Pour the wild rice in a saucepan, then pour in enough water to cover. Bring to a boil.
3. Reduce the heat to low, then simmer for 45 minutes or until the wild rice is soft and plump. Drain and transfer to a large serving bowl.
4. Top the rice with papayas, jicama, peas, cabbage, and scallion. Pour the sauce over and stir to mix well before serving.

Nutrition Info:
- Info Per Serving: Calories: 446;Fat: 7.9g;Protein: 3.1g;Carbs: 85.8g.

Moroccan Rice Pilaf

Servings:4
Cooking Time:40 Minutes
Ingredients:
- 2 tbsp olive oil
- ¼ cup pine nuts
- 1 ¼ cups brown rice
- 1 onion, diced
- 2 cups chicken stock
- 1 cinnamon stick
- ¼ cup dried apricots, chopped
- Salt and black pepper to taste

Directions:

1. Warm the olive oil in a large saucepan over medium heat.
2. Sauté the onions and pine nuts for 5-7 minutes, or until the pine nuts are golden and the onion is translucent. Add the rice and sauté for 2 minutes until lightly browned. Pour the stock and bring it to a boil. Add the cinnamon and apricots.
3. Lower the heat, cover the pan, and simmer for 17-20 minutes or until the rice is tender and the liquid is mostly absorbed. When ready, remove from the heat and fluff with a fork. Season to taste and serve warm.

Nutrition Info:
- Info Per Serving: Calories: 510;Fat: 24g;Protein: 13g;Carbs: 62g.

Roasted Ratatouille Pasta

Servings:2
Cooking Time: 30 Minutes
Ingredients:
- 1 small eggplant
- 1 small zucchini
- 1 portobello mushroom
- 1 Roma tomato, halved
- ½ medium sweet red pepper, seeded
- ½ teaspoon salt, plus additional for the pasta water
- 1 teaspoon Italian herb seasoning
- 1 tablespoon olive oil
- 2 cups farfalle pasta
- 2 tablespoons minced sun-dried tomatoes in olive oil with herbs
- 2 tablespoons prepared pesto

Directions:
1. Slice the ends off the eggplant and zucchini. Cut them lengthwise into ½-inch slices.
2. Place the eggplant, zucchini, mushroom, tomato, and red pepper in a large bowl and sprinkle with ½ teaspoon of salt. Using your hands, toss the vegetables well so that they're covered evenly with the salt. Let them rest for about 10 minutes.
3. While the vegetables are resting, preheat the oven to 400ºF. Line a baking sheet with parchment paper.
4. When the oven is hot, drain off any liquid from the vegetables and pat them dry with a paper towel. Add the Italian herb seasoning and olive oil to the vegetables and toss well to coat both sides.
5. Lay the vegetables out in a single layer on the baking sheet. Roast them for 15 to 20 minutes, flipping them over after about 10 minutes or once they start to brown on the

underside. When the vegetables are charred in spots, remove them from the oven.

6. While the vegetables are roasting, fill a large saucepan with water. Add salt and cook the pasta until al dente, about 8 to 10 minutes. Drain the pasta, reserving ½ cup of the pasta water.

7. When cool enough to handle, cut the vegetables into large chunks and add them to the hot pasta.

8. Stir in the sun-dried tomatoes and pesto and toss everything well. Serve immediately.

Nutrition Info:

- Info Per Serving: Calories: 613;Fat: 16.0g;Protein: 23.1g;Carbs: 108.5g.

Tortellini & Cannellini With Meatballs

Servings:4
Cooking Time:30 Minutes
Ingredients:

- 2 tbsp parsley, chopped
- 12 oz fresh tortellini
- 3 tbsp olive oil
- 5 cloves garlic, minced
- ½ lb meatballs
- 1 can cannellini beans
- 1 can roasted tomatoes
- Salt and black pepper to taste

Directions:

1. Bring to a boil salted water in a pot over high heat. Add the tortellini and cook according to package directions. Drain and set aside. Warm the olive oil in a large skillet over medium heat and sauté the garlic for 1 minute. Stir in meatballs and brown for 4–5 minutes on all sides. Add the tomatoes and cannellini and continue to cook for 5 minutes or until heated through. Adjust the seasoning with salt and pepper. Stir in tortellini. Sprinkle with parsley and serve.

Nutrition Info:

- Info Per Serving: Calories: 578;Fat: 30g;Protein: 25g;Carbs: 58g.

Mediterranean-style Beans And Greens

Servings:2
Cooking Time: 15 Minutes
Ingredients:

- 1 can diced tomatoes with juice
- 1 can cannellini beans, drained and rinsed
- 2 tablespoons chopped green olives, plus 1 or 2 sliced for garnish
- ¼ cup vegetable broth, plus more as needed
- 1 teaspoon extra-virgin olive oil
- 2 cloves garlic, minced
- 4 cups arugula
- ¼ cup freshly squeezed lemon juice

Directions:

1. In a medium saucepan, bring the tomatoes, beans and chopped olives to a low boil, adding just enough broth to make the ingredients saucy (you may need more than ¼ cup if your canned tomatoes don't have a lot of juice). Reduce heat to low and simmer for about 5 minutes.

2. Meanwhile, in a large skillet, heat the olive oil over medium-high heat. When the oil is hot and starts to shimmer, add garlic and sauté just until it starts to turn slightly tan, about 30 seconds. Add the arugula and lemon juice, stirring to coat leaves with the olive oil and juice. Cover and reduce heat to low. Simmer for 3 to 5 minutes.

3. Serve beans over the greens and garnish with olive slices.

Nutrition Info:

- Info Per Serving: Calories: 262;Fat: 5.9g;Protein: 13.2g;Carbs: 40.4g.

Autumn Vegetable & Rigatoni Bake

Servings:6
Cooking Time:45 Minutes
Ingredients:

- 2 tbsp grated Pecorino-Romano cheese
- 2 tbsp olive oil
- 1 lb pumpkin, chopped
- 1 zucchini, chopped
- 1 onion, chopped
- 1 lb rigatoni
- Salt and black pepper to taste
- ½ tsp garlic powder
- ½ cup dry white wine

Directions:

1. Preheat oven to 420 F. Combine zucchini, pumpkin, onion, and olive oil in a bowl. Arrange on a lined aluminum foil sheet and season with salt, pepper, and garlic powder. Bake for 30 minutes until tender. In a pot of boiling water, cook rigatoni for 8-10 minutes until al dente. Drain and set aside.

2. In a food processor, place ½ cup of the roasted veggies and wine and pulse until smooth. Transfer to a skillet over medium heat. Stir in rigatoni and cook until heated through. Top with the remaining vegetables and Pecorino cheese to serve.

Nutrition Info:

- Info Per Serving: Calories: 186;Fat: 11g;Protein: 10g;Carbs: 15g.

Ricotta & Olive Rigatoni

Servings:4
Cooking Time:25 Minutes
Ingredients:

- 2 tbsp extra-virgin olive oil
- 1 lb rigatoni
- ½ lb Ricotta cheese, crumbled
- 3⁄4 cup black olives, chopped
- 10 sun-dried tomatoes, sliced
- 1 tbsp dried oregano
- Black pepper to taste

Directions:

1. Bring to a boil salted water in a pot over high heat. Add the rigatoni and cook according to package directions; drain. Heat the olive oil in a large saucepan over medium heat. Add the rigatoni, ricotta, olives, and sun-dried tomatoes. Toss mixture to combine and cook 2–3 minutes or until cheese just starts to melt. Season with oregano and pepper.

Nutrition Info:

- Info Per Serving: Calories: 383;Fat: 28g;Protein: 15g;Carbs: 21g.

Lemony Green Quinoa

Servings:4
Cooking Time:30 Minutes
Ingredients:

- 2 tbsp olive oil
- 1 onion, chopped
- 2 garlic cloves, minced
- 1 cup quinoa, rinsed
- 1 lb asparagus, chopped
- 2 tbsp fresh parsley, chopped
- 2 tbsp lemon juice
- 1 tsp lemon zest, grated
- ½ lb green beans, trimmed and halved
- Salt and black pepper to taste
- ½ lb cherry tomatoes, halved

Directions:

1. Heat olive oil in a pot over medium heat and sauté onion and garlic for 3 minutes until soft. Stir in quinoa for 1-2 minutes. Pour in 2 cups of water and season with salt and pepper. Bring to a bowl and reduce the heat. Simmer for 5 minutes. Stir in green beans and asparagus and cook for another 10 minutes. Remove from the heat and mix in cherry tomatoes, lemon juice and lemon zest. Top with parsley and serve.

Nutrition Info:

- Info Per Serving: Calories: 430;Fat: 16g;Protein: 17g;Carbs: 60g.

Wild Rice With Cheese & Mushrooms

Servings:4
Cooking Time:30 Minutes
Ingredients:

- 2 cups chicken stock
- 1 cup wild rice
- 1 onion, chopped
- ½ lb wild mushrooms, sliced
- 2 garlic cloves, minced
- 1 lemon, juiced and zested
- 1 tbsp chives, chopped
- ½ cup mozzarella, grated
- Salt and black pepper to taste

Directions:

1. Warm chicken stock in a pot over medium heat and add in wild rice, onion, mushrooms, garlic, lemon juice, lemon zest, salt, and pepper. Bring to a simmer and cook for 20 minutes. Transfer to a baking tray and top with mozzarella cheese. Place the tray under the broiler for 4 minutes until the cheese is melted. Sprinkle with chives and serve.

Nutrition Info:

- Info Per Serving: Calories: 230;Fat: 6g;Protein: 6g;Carbs: 13g.

Bulgur Pilaf With Kale And Tomatoes

Servings:2

Cooking Time: 10 Minutes

Ingredients:

- 2 tablespoons olive oil
- 2 cloves garlic, minced
- 1 bunch kale, trimmed and cut into bite-sized pieces
- Juice of 1 lemon
- 2 cups cooked bulgur wheat
- 1 pint cherry tomatoes, halved
- Sea salt and freshly ground pepper, to taste

Directions:

1. Heat the olive oil in a large skillet over medium heat. Add the garlic and sauté for 1 minute.

2. Add the kale leaves and stir to coat. Cook for 5 minutes until leaves are cooked through and thoroughly wilted.

3. Add the lemon juice, bulgur and tomatoes. Season with sea salt and freshly ground pepper to taste, then serve.

Nutrition Info:

- Info Per Serving: Calories: 300;Fat: 14.0g;Protein: 6.2g;Carbs: 37.8g.

Mozzarella & Asparagus Pasta

Servings:6

Cooking Time:40 Minutes

Ingredients:

- 1 ½ lb asparagus, trimmed, cut into 1-inch
- 2 tbsp olive oil
- 8 oz orecchiette
- 2 cups cherry tomatoes, halved
- Salt and black pepper to taste
- 2 cups fresh mozzarella, drained and chopped
- ⅓ cup torn basil leaves
- 2 tbsp balsamic vinegar

Directions:

1. Preheat oven to 390 F. In a large pot, cook the pasta according to the directions. Drain, reserving ¼ cup of cooking water.

2. In the meantime, in a large bowl, toss in asparagus, cherry tomatoes, oil, pepper, and salt. Spread the mixture onto a rimmed baking sheet and bake for 15 minutes, stirring twice throughout cooking. Remove the veggies from the oven, and add the cooked pasta to the baking sheet. Mix with a few tbsp of pasta water to smooth the sauce and veggies. Slowly mix in the mozzarella and basil. Drizzle with the balsamic vinegar and serve in bowls.

Nutrition Info:

- Info Per Serving: Calories: 188;Fat: 11g;Protein: 14g;Carbs: 23g.

Rigatoni With Peppers & Mozzarella

Servings:4

Cooking Time:30 Min + Marinating Time

Ingredients:

- 1 lb fresh mozzarella cheese, cubed
- 3 tbsp olive oil
- ¼ cup chopped fresh chives
- ¼ cup basil, chopped
- ½ tsp red pepper flakes
- 1 tsp apple cider vinegar
- Salt and black pepper to taste
- 3 garlic cloves, minced
- 2 cups sliced onions
- 3 cups bell peppers, sliced
- 2 cups tomato sauce
- 8 oz rigatoni
- 1 tbsp butter
- ¼ cup grated Parmesan cheese

Directions:

1. Bring to a boil salted water in a pot over high heat. Add the rigatoni and cook according to package directions. Drain and set aside, reserving 1 cup of the cooking water. Combine the mozzarella, 1 tablespoon of olive oil, chives, basil, pepper flakes, apple cider vinegar, salt, and pepper. Let the cheese marinate for 30 minutes at room temperature

2. Warm the remaining olive oil in a large skillet over medium heat. Stir-fry the garlic for 10 seconds and add the onions and peppers. Cook for 3-4 minutes, stirring occasionally until the onions are translucent. Pour in the tomato sauce, and reduce the heat to a simmer. Add the rigatoni and reserved cooking water and toss to coat. Heat off and adjust the seasoning with salt and pepper. Toss with marinated mozzarella cheese and butter. Sprinkle with Parmesan cheese and serve.

Nutrition Info:

- Info Per Serving: Calories: 434;Fat: 18g;Protein: 44g;Carbs: 27g.

Rich Cauliflower Alfredo

Servings:4

Cooking Time: 30 Minutes

Ingredients:

- Cauliflower Alfredo Sauce:
- 1 tablespoon avocado oil
- ½ yellow onion, diced
- 2 cups cauliflower florets
- 2 garlic cloves, minced
- 1½ teaspoons miso
- 1 teaspoon Dijon mustard
- Pinch of ground nutmeg
- ½ cup unsweetened almond milk
- 1½ tablespoons fresh lemon juice
- 2 tablespoons nutritional yeast
- Sea salt and ground black pepper, to taste
- Fettuccine:
- 1 tablespoon avocado oil
- ½ yellow onion, diced
- 1 cup broccoli florets
- 1 zucchini, halved lengthwise and cut into ¼-inch-thick half-moons
- Sea salt and ground black pepper, to taste
- ½ cup sun-dried tomatoes, drained if packed in oil
- 8 ounces cooked whole-wheat fettuccine
- ½ cup fresh basil, cut into ribbons

Directions:

1. Make the Sauce:
2. Heat the avocado oil in a nonstick skillet over medium-high heat until shimmering.
3. Add half of the onion to the skillet and sauté for 5 minutes or until translucent.
4. Add the cauliflower and garlic to the skillet. Reduce the heat to low and cook for 8 minutes or until the cauliflower is tender.
5. Pour them in a food processor, add the remaining ingredients for the sauce and pulse to combine well. Set aside.
6. Make the Fettuccine:
7. Heat the avocado oil in a nonstick skillet over medium-high heat.
8. Add the remaining half of onion and sauté for 5 minutes or until translucent.
9. Add the broccoli and zucchini. Sprinkle with salt and ground black pepper, then sauté for 5 minutes or until tender.
10. Add the sun-dried tomatoes, reserved sauce, and fettuccine. Sauté for 3 minutes or until well-coated and heated through.
11. Serve the fettuccine on a large plate and spread with basil before serving.

Nutrition Info:

- Info Per Serving: Calories: 288;Fat: 15.9g;Protein: 10.1g;Carbs: 32.5g.

Lush Moroccan Chickpea, Vegetable, And Fruit Stew

Servings:6

Cooking Time: 6 Hours 4 Minutes

Ingredients:

- 1 large bell pepper, any color, chopped
- 6 ounces green beans, trimmed and cut into bite-size pieces
- 3 cups canned chickpeas, rinsed and drained
- 1 can diced tomatoes, with the juice
- 1 large carrot, cut into ¼-inch rounds
- 2 large potatoes, peeled and cubed
- 1 large yellow onion, chopped
- 1 teaspoon grated fresh ginger
- 2 garlic cloves, minced
- 1¾ cups low-sodium vegetable soup
- 1 teaspoon ground cumin
- 1 tablespoon ground coriander
- ¼ teaspoon ground red pepper flakes
- Sea salt and ground black pepper, to taste
- 8 ounces fresh baby spinach
- ¼ cup diced dried figs
- ¼ cup diced dried apricots
- 1 cup plain Greek yogurt

Directions:

1. Place the bell peppers, green beans, chicken peas, tomatoes and juice, carrot, potatoes, onion, ginger, and garlic in the slow cooker.
2. Pour in the vegetable soup and sprinkle with cumin, coriander, red pepper flakes, salt, and ground black pepper. Stir to mix well.
3. Put the slow cooker lid on and cook on high for 6 hours or until the vegetables are soft. Stir periodically.
4. Open the lid and fold in the spinach, figs, apricots, and yogurt. Stir to mix well.
5. Cook for 4 minutes or until the spinach is wilted. Pour them in a large serving bowl. Allow to cool for at least 20 minutes, then serve warm.

One-step Couscous

Servings:6

Cooking Time:15 Minutes

Ingredients:

• 2 tbsp olive oil

• 2 cups couscous

• 1 cup water

• 1 cup vegetable broth

• Salt and black pepper to taste

Directions:

1. In a saucepan, heat the oil and add couscous. Stir until grains are just almost brown, 3-5 minutes. Stir in water, broth, and one teaspoon salt. Cover, remove the saucepan from the heat, and let sit until couscous is tender, 7 minutes. Gently fluff couscous with fork and season with pepper to taste.

Nutrition Info:

• Info Per Serving: Calories: 355;Fat: 6g;Protein: 8g;Carbs: 44g.

Chickpea Salad With Tomatoes And Basil

Servings:2

Cooking Time: 45 Minutes

Ingredients:

• 1 cup dried chickpeas, rinsed

• 1 quart water, or enough to cover the chickpeas by 3 to 4 inches

• 1½ cups halved grape tomatoes

• 1 cup chopped fresh basil leaves

• 2 to 3 tablespoons balsamic vinegar

• ½ teaspoon garlic powder

• ½ teaspoon salt, plus more as needed

Directions:

1. In your Instant Pot, combine the chickpeas and water.

2. Secure the lid. Select the Manual mode and set the cooking time for 45 minutes at High Pressure.

3. Once cooking is complete, do a natural pressure release for 20 minutes, then release any remaining pressure. Carefully open the lid and drain the chickpeas. Refrigerate to cool (unless you want to serve this warm, which is good, too).

4. While the chickpeas cool, in a large bowl, stir together the basil, tomatoes, vinegar, garlic powder, and salt. Add the beans, stir to combine, and serve.

Nutrition Info:

• Info Per Serving: Calories: 395;Fat: 6.0g;Protein: 19.8g;Carbs: 67.1g.

Fruits, Desserts And Snacks Recipes

Sicilian Almond Granita

Servings:4
Cooking Time:5 Min + Freezing Time
Ingredients:

- 4 small oranges, chopped
- ½ tsp almond extract
- 2 tbsp lemon juice
- 1 cup orange juice
- ¼ cup honey
- Fresh mint leaves for garnish

Directions:

1. In a food processor, mix oranges, orange juice, honey, almond extract, and lemon juice. Pulse until smooth. Pour in a dip dish and freeze for 1 hour. Mix with a fork and freeze for 30 minutes more. Repeat a couple of times. Pour into dessert glasses and garnish with basil leaves. Serve.

Nutrition Info:

- Info Per Serving: Calories: 145;Fat: 0g;Protein: 1.5g;Carbs: 36g.

Berry And Rhubarb Cobbler

Servings:8
Cooking Time: 35 Minutes
Ingredients:

- Cobbler:
- 1 cup fresh raspberries
- 2 cups fresh blueberries
- 1 cup sliced (½-inch) rhubarb pieces
- 1 tablespoon arrowroot powder
- ¼ cup unsweetened apple juice
- 2 tablespoons melted coconut oil
- ¼ cup raw honey
- Topping:
- 1 cup almond flour
- 1 tablespoon arrowroot powder
- ½ cup shredded coconut
- ¼ cup raw honey
- ½ cup coconut oil

Directions:

1. Make the Cobbler
2. Preheat the oven to 350ºF. Grease a baking dish with melted coconut oil.

3. Combine the ingredients for the cobbler in a large bowl. Stir to mix well.
4. Spread the mixture in the single layer on the baking dish. Set aside.
5. Make the Topping
6. Combine the almond flour, arrowroot powder, and coconut in a bowl. Stir to mix well.
7. Fold in the honey and coconut oil. Stir with a fork until the mixture crumbled.
8. Spread the topping over the cobbler, then bake in the preheated oven for 35 minutes or until frothy and golden brown.
9. Serve immediately.

Nutrition Info:

- Info Per Serving: Calories: 305;Fat: 22.1g;Protein: 3.2g;Carbs: 29.8g.

Turkish Baklava

Servings:6
Cooking Time:40 Min + Chilling Time
Ingredients:

- 20 sheets phyllo pastry dough, at room temperature
- 1 cup butter, melted
- 1 ½ cups chopped walnuts
- 1 tsp ground cinnamon
- ¼ tsp ground cardamom
- ½ cup sugar
- ½ cup honey
- 2 tbsp lemon juice
- 1 tbsp lemon zest

Directions:

1. In a small pot, bring 1 cup of water, sugar, honey, lemon zest, and lemon juice just to a boil. Remove and let cool.
2. Preheat oven to 350 F. In a small bowl, mix the walnuts, cinnamon, and cardamom and set aside. Put the butter in a small bowl. Put 1 layer of phyllo dough on a baking sheet and slowly brush with butter. Carefully layer 2 more phyllo sheets, brushing each with butter in the baking pan and then layer 1 tbsp of the nut mix; layer 2 sheets and add another 1 tbsp of the nut mix; repeat with 2 sheets and nuts until you run out of nuts and dough, topping with the remaining phyllo dough sheets. Slice 4 lines into the baklava lengthwise and make another 4 or 5 slices diagonally across the pan. Bake for 30-40 minutes or until golden brown.

Remove the baklava from the oven and immediately cover it with the syrup. Let cool and serve.

Nutrition Info:

- Info Per Serving: Calories: 443;Fat: 27g;Protein: 6g;Carbs: 47g.

Hot Italian Sausage Pizza Wraps

Servings:2

Cooking Time:20 Minutes

Ingredients:

- 1 tbsp basil, chopped
- 1 tsp olive oil
- 6 oz spicy Italian sausage
- 1 shallot, chopped
- 1 tsp Italian seasoning
- 4 oz marinara sauce
- 2 flour tortillas
- ½ cup mozzarella, shredded
- 1/3 cup Parmesan, grated
- 1 tsp red pepper flakes

Directions:

1. Warm the olive oil in a skillet over medium heat. Add and cook the sausage for 5-6 minutes, stirring and breaking up larger pieces, until cooked through. Remove to a bowl. Sauté the shallot for 3 minutes until soft, stirring frequently. Stir in Italian seasoning, marinara sauce, and reserved sausage. Bring to a simmer and cook for about 2 minutes. Divide the mixture between the tortillas, top with the cheeses, add red pepper flakes and basil, and fold over. Serve immediately.

Nutrition Info:

- Info Per Serving: Calories: 744;Fat: 46g;Protein: 41g;Carbs: 40g.

Kid´s Marzipan Balls

Servings:6

Cooking Time:10 Minutes

Ingredients:

- ½ cup avocado oil
- 1 ½ cup almond flour
- ½ cup sugar
- 2 tsp almond extract

Directions:

1. Add the almond flour and sugar and pulse to your food processor until the mixture is ground. Add the almond extract and pulse until combined. With the processor running, stream in oil until the mixture starts to form a large ball. Turn off the food processor. With hands, form the marzipan into six 1-inch diameter balls. Press to hold the mixture together. Store in an airtight container in the refrigerator for up to 14 days.

Nutrition Info:

- Info Per Serving: Calories: 157;Fat: 17g;Protein: 2g;Carbs: 0g.

Coconut Blueberries With Brown Rice

Servings:4

Cooking Time: 10 Minutes

Ingredients:

- 1 cup fresh blueberries
- 2 cups unsweetened coconut milk
- 1 teaspoon ground ginger
- ¼ cup maple syrup
- Sea salt, to taste
- 2 cups cooked brown rice

Directions:

1. Put all the ingredients, except for the brown rice, in a pot. Stir to combine well.

2. Cook over medium-high heat for 7 minutes or until the blueberries are tender.

3. Pour in the brown rice and cook for 3 more minute or until the rice is soft. Stir constantly.

4. Serve immediately.

Nutrition Info:

- Info Per Serving: Calories: 470;Fat: 24.8g;Protein: 6.2g;Carbs: 60.1g.

Cucumber Sticks With Dill-cheese Dip

Servings:4

Cooking Time:10 Minutes

Ingredients:

- 3 cucumbers, julienned and deseeded
- ¼ cup olive oil
- ¼ tsp salt
- 1 garlic clove, minced
- 2 tbsp dill, chopped
- ¼ cup grated Parmesan cheese
- ¼ cup almonds, chopped
- ½ tsp paprika

Directions:

1. Season cucumbers and arrange on a platter. Mix dill, almonds, garlic, Parmesan cheese, and olive oil in a food processor until smooth. Spoon the dip over the cucumbers and season with paprika to serve.

Nutrition Info:

- Info Per Serving: Calories: 182;Fat: 16g;Protein: 4g;Carbs: 10g.

Salty Spicy Popcorn

Servings:6
Cooking Time:10 Minutes
Ingredients:

- 3 tbsp olive oil
- ¼ tsp garlic powder
- Salt and black pepper to taste
- ½ tsp dried thyme
- ½ tsp chili powder
- ½ tsp dried oregano
- 12 cups plain popped popcorn

Directions:

1. Warm the olive oil in a large pan over medium heat. Add the garlic powder, black pepper, salt, chili powder, thyme, and stir oregano until fragrant, 1 minute. Place the popcorn in a large bowl and drizzle with the infused oil over. Toss to coat.

Nutrition Info:

- Info Per Serving: Calories: 183;Fat: 12g;Protein: 4g;Carbs: 19g.

Baby Artichoke Antipasto

Servings:4
Cooking Time:5 Minutes
Ingredients:

- 1 jar roasted red peppers
- 8 canned artichoke hearts
- 1 can garbanzo beans
- 1 cup whole Kalamata olives
- ¼ cup balsamic vinegar
- Salt to taste
- 1 lemon, zested

Directions:

1. Slice the peppers and put them into a large bowl. Cut the artichoke hearts into quarters, and add them to the bowl. Add the garbanzo beans, olives, balsamic vinegar, lemon zest, and salt. Toss all the ingredients together. Serve chilled.

Nutrition Info:

- Info Per Serving: Calories: 281;Fat: 15g;Protein: 7g;Carbs: 30g.

Spicy Chorizo Pizza

Servings:4
Cooking Time:45 Minutes
Ingredients:

- For the crust
- 2 tbsp olive oil
- 2 cups flour
- 1 cup lukewarm water
- 1 pinch of sugar
- 1 tsp active dry yeast
- ¾ tsp salt
- For the topping
- 1 cup sliced smoked mozzarella cheese
- 1 tbsp olive oil
- 1 cups sliced chorizo
- ¼ cup marinara sauce
- 1 jalapeño pepper, sliced
- ¼ red onion, thinly sliced

Directions:

1. Sift the flour and salt in a bowl and stir in yeast. Mix lukewarm water, olive oil, and sugar in another bowl. Add the wet mixture to the dry mixture and whisk until you obtain a soft dough. Place the dough on a lightly floured work surface and knead it thoroughly for 4-5 minutes until elastic. Transfer the dough to a greased bowl. Cover with cling film and leave to rise for 50-60 minutes in a warm place until doubled in size. Roll out the dough to a thickness of around 12 inches.

2. Preheat the oven to 400 F. Line a pizza pan with parchment paper. Heat the olive oil and cook the chorizo until brown, 5 minutes. Spread the marinara sauce on the crust, top with the mozzarella cheese, chorizo, jalapeño pepper, and onion. Bake in the oven until the cheese melts, 15 minutes. Remove from the oven, slice, and serve warm.

Nutrition Info:

- Info Per Serving: Calories: 391;Fat: 17g;Protein: 11g;Carbs: 51g.

Simple Apple Compote

Servings:4

Cooking Time: 10 Minutes

Ingredients:

- 6 apples, peeled, cored, and chopped
- ¼ cup raw honey
- 1 teaspoon ground cinnamon
- ¼ cup apple juice
- Sea salt, to taste

Directions:

1. Put all the ingredients in a stockpot. Stir to mix well, then cook over medium-high heat for 10 minutes or until the apples are glazed by honey and lightly saucy. Stir constantly.

2. Serve immediately.

Nutrition Info:

- Info Per Serving: Calories: 246;Fat: 0.9g;Protein: 1.2g;Carbs: 66.3g.

Charred Asparagus

Servings:4

Cooking Time:25 Minutes

Ingredients:

- 2 tbsp olive oil
- 1 lb asparagus, trimmed
- 4 tbsp Grana Padano, grated
- ½ tsp garlic powder
- Salt to taste
- 2 tbsp parsley, chopped

Directions:

1. Preheat the grill to high. Season the asparagus with salt and garlic powder and coat with olive oil. Grill the asparagus for 10 minutes, turning often until lightly charred and tender. Sprinkle with cheese and parsley and serve.

Nutrition Info:

- Info Per Serving: Calories: 105;Fat: 8g;Protein: 4.3g;Carbs: 4.7g.

Chocolate And Avocado Mousse

Servings:4

Cooking Time: 5 Minutes

Ingredients:

- 8 ounces dark chocolate, chopped
- ¼ cup unsweetened coconut milk
- 2 tablespoons coconut oil
- 2 ripe avocados, deseeded
- ¼ cup raw honey
- Sea salt, to taste

Directions:

1. Put the chocolate in a saucepan. Pour in the coconut milk and add the coconut oil.

2. Cook for 3 minutes or until the chocolate and coconut oil melt. Stir constantly.

3. Put the avocado in a food processor, then drizzle with honey and melted chocolate. Pulse to combine until smooth

4. Pour the mixture in a serving bowl, then sprinkle with salt. Refrigerate to chill for 30 minutes and serve.

Nutrition Info:

- Info Per Serving: Calories: 654;Fat: 46.8g;Protein 7.2g;Carbs: 55.9g.

Pecan & Raspberry & Frozen Yogurt Cups

Servings:4

Cooking Time:10 Minutes

Ingredients:

- 2 cups fresh raspberries
- 4 cups vanilla frozen yogurt
- 1 lime, zested
- ¼ cup chopped praline pecans

Directions:

1. Divide the frozen yogurt into 4 dessert glasses. Top with raspberries, lime zest, and pecans. Serve immediately.

Nutrition Info:

- Info Per Serving: Calories: 142;Fat: 3.4g;Protein 3.7g;Carbs: 26g.

Mint-watermelon Gelato

Servings:4
Cooking Time:10 Min + Freezing Time
Ingredients:

- ¼ cup honey
- 4 cups watermelon cubes
- ¼ cup lemon juice
- 12 mint leaves to serve

Directions:

1. In a food processor, blend the watermelon, honey, and lemon juice to form a purée with chunks. Transfer to a freezer-proof container and place in the freezer for 1 hour.

2. Remove the container from and scrape with a fork. Return the to the freezer and repeat the process every half hour until the sorbet is completely frozen, for around 4 hours. Share into bowls, garnish with mint leaves, and serve.

Nutrition Info:

- Info Per Serving: Calories: 149;Fat: 0.4g;Protein: 1.8g;Carbs: 38g.

Goat Cheese Dip With Scallions & Lemon

Servings:4
Cooking Time:10 Minutes
Ingredients:

- 2 tbsp extra virgin olive oil
- 2 oz goat cheese, crumbled
- ¾ cup sour cream
- 2 tbsp scallions, chopped
- 1 tbsp lemon juice
- Salt and black pepper to taste

Directions:

1. Combine goat cheese, sour cream, scallions, lemon juice, salt, pepper, and olive oil in a bowl and transfer to the fridge for 10 minutes before serving.

Nutrition Info:

- Info Per Serving: Calories: 230;Fat: 12g;Protein: 6g;Carbs: 9g.

Healthy Tuna Stuffed Zucchini Rolls

Servings:4
Cooking Time:5 Minutes
Ingredients:

- 5 oz canned tuna, drained and mashed
- 2 tbsp olive oil
- ½ cup mayonnaise
- 2 tbsp capers
- 2 zucchinis, sliced lengthwise
- Salt and black pepper to taste
- 1 tsp lime juice

Directions:

1. Heat a grill pan over medium heat. Drizzle the zucchini slices with olive oil and season with salt and pepper. Grill for 5-6 minutes on both sides. In a bowl, mix the tuna, capers, lime juice, mayonnaise, salt, and pepper until well combined. Spread the tuna mixture onto zucchini slices and roll them up. Transfer the rolls to a plate and serve.

Nutrition Info:

- Info Per Serving: Calories: 210;Fat: 7g;Protein: 4g;Carbs: 8g.

Cardamom Apple Slices

Servings:2
Cooking Time:30 Minutes
Ingredients:

- 1 ½ tsp cardamom
- ½ tsp salt
- 4 peeled, cored apples, sliced
- 2 tbsp honey
- 2 tbsp milk

Directions:

1. Preheat oven to 390 F. In a bowl, combine apple slices, salt, and ½ tsp of cardamom. Arrange them on a greased baking dish and cook for 20 minutes. Remove to a serving plate.

2. In the meantime, place milk, honey, and remaining cardamom in a pot over medium heat. Cook until simmer. Pour the sauce over the apples and serve immediately.

Nutrition Info:

- Info Per Serving: Calories: 287;Fat: 3g;Protein: 2g;Carbs: 69g.

Bruschetta With Tomato & Basil

Servings:4
Cooking Time:20 Minutes
Ingredients:
- 1 ciabatta loaf, halved lengthwise
- 2 tbsp olive oil
- 3 tbsp basil, chopped
- 4 tomatoes, cubed
- 1 shallot, sliced
- 2 garlic cloves, minced
- Salt and black pepper to taste
- 1 tbsp balsamic vinegar
- ½ tsp garlic powder

Directions:
1. Preheat the oven to 380 F. Line a baking sheet with parchment paper. Cut in half each half of the ciabatta loaf. Place them on the sheet and sprinkle with some olive oil. Bake for 10 minutes. Mix tomatoes, shallot, basil, garlic, salt, pepper, olive oil, vinegar, and garlic powder in a bowl and let sit for 10 minutes. Apportion the mixture among bread pieces.

Nutrition Info:
- Info Per Serving: Calories: 170;Fat: 5g;Protein: 5g;Carbs: 30g.

Salmon-cucumber Rolls

Servings:4
Cooking Time:5 Minutes
Ingredients:
- 8 Kalamata olives, chopped
- 4 oz smoked salmon strips
- 1 cucumber, sliced lengthwise
- 2 tsp lime juice
- 4 oz cream cheese, soft
- 1 tsp lemon zest, grated
- Salt and black pepper to taste
- 2 tsp dill, chopped

Directions:
1. Place cucumber slices on a flat surface and top each with a salmon strip. Combine olives, lime juice, cream cheese, lemon zest, salt, pepper, and dill in a bowl. Smear cream mixture over salmon and roll them up. Serve immediately.

Nutrition Info:
- Info Per Serving: Calories: 250;Fat: 16g;Protein: 18g;Carbs: 17g.

Mascarpone Baked Pears

Servings:2
Cooking Time: 20 Minutes
Ingredients:
- 2 ripe pears, peeled
- 1 tablespoon plus 2 teaspoons honey, divided
- 1 teaspoon vanilla, divided
- ¼ teaspoon ground coriander
- ¼ teaspoon ginger
- ¼ cup minced walnuts
- ¼ cup mascarpone cheese
- Pinch salt
- Cooking spray

Directions:
1. Preheat the oven to 350ºF. Spray a small baking dish with cooking spray.
2. Slice the pears in half lengthwise. Using a spoon, scoop out the core from each piece. Put the pears, cut side up, in the baking dish.
3. Whisk together 1 tablespoon of honey, ½ teaspoon of vanilla, ginger, and coriander in a small bowl. Pour this mixture evenly over the pear halves.
4. Scatter the walnuts over the pear halves.
5. Bake in the preheated oven for 20 minutes, or until the pears are golden and you're able to pierce them easily with a knife.
6. Meanwhile, combine the mascarpone cheese with the remaining 2 teaspoons of honey, ½ teaspoon of vanilla, and a pinch of salt. Stir to combine well.
7. Divide the mascarpone among the warm pear halves and serve.

Nutrition Info:
- Info Per Serving: Calories: 308;Fat: 16.0g;Protein 4.1g;Carbs: 42.7g.

Fig & Mascarpone Toasts With Pistachios

Servings:6
Cooking Time:10 Minutes
Ingredients:
- 4 tbsp butter, melted
- 1 French baguette, sliced
- 1 cup Mascarpone cheese
- 1 jar fig jam
- ½ cup crushed pistachios

Directions:

1. Preheat oven to 350 F. Arrange the sliced bread on a greased baking sheet and brush each slice with melted butter.

2. Toast the bread for 5-7 minutes until golden brown. Let the bread cool slightly. Spread about a teaspoon of the mascarpone cheese on each piece of bread. Top with fig jam and pistachios.

Nutrition Info:

- Info Per Serving: Calories: 445;Fat: 24g;Protein: 3g;Carbs: 48g.

Cantaloupe & Watermelon Balls

Servings:4

Cooking Time:5 Min + Chilling Time

Ingredients:

- 2 cups watermelon balls
- 2 cups cantaloupe balls
- ½ cup orange juice
- ¼ cup lemon juice
- 1 tbsp orange zest

Directions:

1. Place the watermelon and cantaloupe in a bowl. In another bowl, mix the lemon juice, orange juice and zest. Pour over the fruit. Transfer to the fridge covered for 5 hours. Serve.

Nutrition Info:

- Info Per Serving: Calories: 71;Fat: 0g;Protein: 1.5g;Carbs: 18g.

Eggplant & Pepper Spread On Toasts

Servings:4

Cooking Time:10 Minutes

Ingredients:

- 1 red bell pepper, roasted and chopped
- 1 lb eggplants, baked, peeled and chopped
- ¾ cup olive oil
- 1 lemon, zested
- 1 red chili pepper, chopped
- 1 ½ tsp capers
- 1 garlic clove, minced
- Salt and black pepper to taste
- 1 baguette, sliced and toasted

Directions:

1. In a food processor, place the eggplants, lemon zest, red chili pepper, bell pepper, garlic, salt, and pepper. Blend while gradually adding the olive oil until smooth. Spread

each baguette slice with the spread and top with capers to serve.

Nutrition Info:

- Info Per Serving: Calories: 364;Fat: 38g;Protein: 1.5g;Carbs: 9.3g.

Olive & Caper Olives

Servings:4

Cooking Time:5 Min + Chilling Time

Ingredients:

- ¼ cup extra-virgin olive oil
- 1 ½ cups green olives,
- ½ cup capers
- ½ red onion, sliced
- 3 garlic cloves, minced
- ¼ cup red wine vinegar
- 1 tbsp chopped fresh oregano
- 1 lemon, zested
- ½ tsp sea salt

Directions:

1. Combine olive oil, vinegar, garlic, oregano, lemon zest, and salt in a bowl. Place red onion, olives, and capers in a bowl and pour over the marinade mixture. Serve chilled.

Nutrition Info:

- Info Per Serving: Calories: 261;Fat: 27.2g;Protein: 1.5g;Carbs: 7g.

Country Pizza

Servings:4

Cooking Time:45 Minutes

Ingredients:

- For the crust
- 2 tbsp olive oil
- 2 cups flour
- 1 cup lukewarm water
- 1 pinch of sugar
- 1 tsp active dry yeast
- ¾ tsp salt
- For the ranch sauce
- 1 tbsp butter
- 2 garlic cloves, minced
- 1 tbsp cream cheese
- ¼ cup half and half
- 1 tbsp Ranch seasoning mix
- For the topping
- 3 bacon slices, chopped

- 2 chicken breasts
- Salt and black pepper to taste
- 1 cup grated mozzarella
- 6 fresh basil leaves

Directions:

1. Sift the flour and salt in a bowl and stir in yeast. Mix lukewarm water, olive oil, and sugar in another bowl. Add the wet mixture to the dry mixture and whisk until you obtain a soft dough. Place the dough on a lightly floured work surface and knead it thoroughly for 4-5 minutes until elastic. Transfer the dough to a greased bowl. Cover with cling film and leave to rise for 50-60 minutes in a warm place until doubled in size. Roll out the dough to a thickness of around 12 inches.

2. Preheat the oven to 400 F. Line a pizza pan with parchment paper. In a bowl, mix the sauce's ingredients butter, garlic, cream cheese, half and half, and ranch mix. Set aside. Heat a grill pan over medium heat and cook the bacon until crispy and brown, 5 minutes. Transfer to a plate and set aside.

3. Season the chicken with salt, pepper and grill in the pan on both sides until golden brown, 10 minutes. Remove to a plate, allow cooling and cut into thin slices. Spread the ranch sauce on the pizza crust, followed by the chicken and bacon, and then, mozzarella cheese and basil. Bake for 5 minutes or until the cheese melts. Slice and serve warm.

Nutrition Info:

- Info Per Serving: Calories: 528;Fat: 28g;Protein: 61g;Carbs: 5g.

Lovely Coconut-covered Strawberries

Servings:4
Cooking Time:15 Min + Cooling Time

Ingredients:

- 1 cup chocolate chips
- ¼ cup coconut flakes
- 1 lb strawberries
- ½ tsp vanilla extract
- ½ tsp ground nutmeg
- ¼ tsp salt

Directions:

1. Melt chocolate chips for 30 seconds. Remove and stir in vanilla, nutmeg, and salt. Let cool for 2-3 minutes. Dip strawberries into the chocolate and then into the coconut flakes. Place on a wax paper-lined cookie sheet and let sit for 30 minutes until the chocolate dries. Serve.

Nutrition Info:

- Info Per Serving: Calories: 275;Fat: 20g;Protein 6g;Carbs: 21g.

Pecan And Carrot Cake

Servings:12
Cooking Time: 45 Minutes

Ingredients:

- ½ cup coconut oil, at room temperature, plus more for greasing the baking dish
- 2 teaspoons pure vanilla extract
- ¼ cup pure maple syrup
- 6 eggs
- ½ cup coconut flour
- 1 teaspoon baking powder
- 1 teaspoon baking soda
- ½ teaspoon ground nutmeg
- 1 teaspoon ground cinnamon
- ⅛ teaspoon sea salt
- ½ cup chopped pecans
- 3 cups finely grated carrots

Directions:

1. Preheat the oven to 350ºF. Grease a 13-by-9-inch baking dish with coconut oil.

2. Combine the vanilla extract, maple syrup, and ½ cup of coconut oil in a large bowl. Stir to mix well.

3. Break the eggs in the bowl and whisk to combine well. Set aside.

4. Combine the coconut flour, baking powder, baking soda, nutmeg, cinnamon, and salt in a separate bowl. Stir to mix well.

5. Make a well in the center of the flour mixture, then pour the egg mixture into the well. Stir to combine well.

6. Add the pecans and carrots to the bowl and toss to mix well. Pour the mixture in the single layer on the baking dish

7. Bake in the preheated oven for 45 minutes or until puffed and the cake spring back when lightly press with your fingers.

8. Remove the cake from the oven. Allow to cool for at least 15 minutes, then serve.

Nutrition Info:

- Info Per Serving: Calories: 255;Fat: 21.2g;Protein: 5.1g;Carbs: 12.8g.

Vegetarian Patties

Servings:4
Cooking Time:20 Minutes
Ingredients:

- 3 tbsp olive oil
- 2 carrots, grated
- 2 zucchinis, grated and drained
- 2 garlic cloves, minced
- 2 spring onions, chopped
- 1 tsp cumin
- ½ tsp turmeric powder
- Salt and black pepper to taste
- ¼ tsp ground coriander
- 2 tbsp parsley, chopped
- ¼ tsp lemon juice
- ½ cup flour
- 1 egg, whisked
- ¼ cup breadcrumbs

Directions:

1. Combine garlic, spring onions, carrot, cumin, turmeric, salt, pepper, coriander, parsley, lemon juice, flour, zucchinis, egg, and breadcrumbs in a bowl and mix well. Form balls out of the mixture and flatten them to form patties.

2. Warm olive oil in a skillet over medium heat. Fry the cakes for 10 minutes on both sides. Remove to a paper-lined plate to drain the excessive grease. Serve warm.

Nutrition Info:

- Info Per Serving: Calories: 220;Fat: 12g;Protein: 5g;Carbs: 5g.

Dates Stuffed With Mascarpone & Almonds

Servings:6
Cooking Time:10 Minutes
Ingredients:

- 20 blanched almonds
- 8 oz mascarpone cheese
- 20 Medjool dates
- 2 tbsp honey

Directions:

1. Using a knife, cut one side of the date lengthwise from the stem to the bottom. Gently remove the stone and replace it with a blanched almond. Spoon the cheese into a piping bag. Squeeze a generous amount of the cheese into each date. Set the dates on a serving plate and drizzle with honey. Serve immediately or chill in the fridge.

Nutrition Info:

- Info Per Serving: Calories: 253;Fat: 15g;Protein: 2g;Carbs: 31g.

Appendix : Recipes Index

Cauliflower Steaks With Arugula 37

Charred Asparagus 66

Cheesy Sage Farro 53

Cherry & Pine Nut Couscous 44

Chicken & Barley Soup 44

Chicken Breasts In White Sauce 22

Chicken Bruschetta Burgers 18

Chicken With Bell Peppers 20

Chickpea Salad With Tomatoes And Basil 62

Chili Lentil Soup 49

Chilled Soup With Prawns 51

Chocolate And Avocado Mousse 66

Cilantro Turkey Penne With Asparagus 21

Classic Falafel 52

Classic Potato Salad With Green Onions 49

Classic Shakshuka 10

Coconut Blueberries With Brown Rice 64

Coriander Pork Roast 22

Country Pizza 69

Creamy Cauliflower Chickpea Curry 41

Creamy Peach Smoothie 9

Crispy Sole Fillets 25

Crustless Tiropita (greek Cheese Pie) 6

Cucumber & Spelt Salad With Chicken 46

Cucumber Sticks With Dill-cheese Dip 64

Cumin Cauli Mash 51

D

Date & Hazelnut Crusted Barramundi 26

Dates Stuffed With Mascarpone & Almonds 71

Dill Smoked Salmon & Eggplant Rolls 31

Drunken Lamb Bake 23

E

Easy Breaded Shrimp 32

Easy Roasted Cauliflower 48

Effortless Bell Pepper Salad 45

Egg Bake 10

Eggplant & Chicken Skillet 22

Eggplant & Pepper Spread On Toasts 69

Eggplant Rolls In Tomato Sauce 39

Eggplant, Spinach, And Feta Sandwiches 12

Eggs Florentine With Pancetta 11

Energy Nut Smoothie 15

F

Farro & Trout Bowls With Avocado 31

Fennel Beef Ribs 23

Feta & Zucchini Rosti Cakes 43

Fig & Mascarpone Toasts With Pistachios 68

Fish & Chickpea Stew 36

Fried Eggplant Rolls 36

G

Garlic Shrimp With Arugula Pesto 29

Garlic Skillet Salmon 33

Garlic-butter Asparagus With Parmesan 40

Goat Cheese & Beet Salad With Nuts 50

Goat Cheese Dip With Scallions & Lemon 67

Greek-style Chicken With Potatoes 18

Greek-style Eggplants 37

Greek-style Veggie & Beef In Pita 21

Green Garden Salad 48

Green Veggie & Turkey 19

Grilled Caesar Salad Sandwiches 12

Grilled Chicken Breasts With Italian Sauce 21

Grilled Romaine Lettuce 43

Grilled Za´atar Zucchini Rounds 35

H

Hake Fillet In Herby Tomato Sauce 28

Harissa Turkey With Couscous 19

Hazelnut Crusted Sea Bass 32

Healthy Tuna Stuffed Zucchini Rolls 67

Hearty Veggie Slaw 49

Herby Cod Skewers 27

Herby Tuna Gratin 28

Homemade Pizza Burgers 17

Homemade Vegetarian Moussaka 41

Horiatiki Salad (greek Salad) 45

Hot Italian Sausage Pizza Wraps 64

I

Instant Pot Poached Salmon 25

Israeli Style Eggplant And Chickpea Salad 52

K

Kale-proscuitto Porridge 14

Kid´s Marzipan Balls 64

Pesto Ravioli Salad 47
Pesto Salami & Cheese Egg Cupcakes 13
Pesto Shrimp Over Zoodles 25
Pork Chops In Tomato Olive Sauce 18
Portuguese Thyme & Mushroom Millet 55
Potato Tortilla With Leeks And Mushrooms 35

Q

Quick Za´atar Spice 47
Quinoa & Watercress Salad With Nuts 53

R

Rich Cauliflower Alfredo 61
Ricotta & Olive Rigatoni 59
Ricotta Muffins With Pear Glaze 8
Rigatoni With Peppers & Mozzarella 60
Roasted Celery Root With Yogurt Sauce 34
Roasted Ratatouille Pasta 57
Roasted Vegetable Panini 9
Roasted Vegetables 40
Roasted Vegetables And Chickpeas 37

S

Salmon & Curly Endive Salad 44
Salmon Packets 30
Salmon-cucumber Rolls 68
Salty Spicy Popcorn 65
Sausage & Herb Eggs 24
Savory Tomato Chicken 20
Seared Salmon With Lemon Cream Sauce 26
Shrimp And Pea Paella 29
Shrimp Quinoa Bowl With Black Olives 33
Sicilian Almond Granita 63
Simple Apple Compote 66
Slow Cook Lamb Shanks With Cannellini Beans Stew 20
Slow Cooker Brussel Sprout & Chicken 23
Slow Cooker Salmon In Foil 25
Smoky Turkey Bake 16
Spanish Chorizo & Spicy Lentil Stew 48
Spiced Citrus Sole 29
Spicy Chorizo Pizza 65
Spicy Mustard Pork Tenderloin 19
Spinach & Bean Salad With Black Olives 45
Spinach & Lentil Stew 41
Spinach & Salmon Fettuccine In White Sauce 56
Summer Gazpacho 51

Made in the USA
Las Vegas, NV
18 September 2023

77726787R00050